REINVENTING
EDUCATION

A 'Thought Experiment'
by 21 authors

Edited by
Vincent Nolan and Gerard Darby

Published by
Synectics Education Initiative (SEI)
13 Marsh Lane, Stoke Mandeville
Buckinghamshire HP22 5UZ

A CIP catalogue record for this title
is available from the British Library

ISBN 0-9538534-1-1

CONTENTS

REINVENTING EDUCATION

Vincent Nolan
Gerard Darby

Editors' Introduction

This book is a collective Thought Experiment, to use Einstein's term. Einstein declared that "Imagination is more important than knowledge". Thought experiments free the mind from pre-conceptions and unconscious assumptions that restrict it.

The original brief for this book asked:

"How would we meet the educational needs of the next half-century, if we were starting from scratch today, unconstrained by existing institutions, systems, beliefs and assumptions? Would we invent schools, colleges and universities, teachers, lecturers, tests and examinations, Ofsted, Qualifications and Curriculum Authority, the Teacher Training Agency and the rest? Would we invent Local Education Authorities and the Department for Education and Science?

Perhaps we would, but the existing state system has grown like Topsy over the last 150 years, with periodic attempts (1870, 1902, 1944 and more recent piecemeal legislation) to adapt the system to the rapidly changing society it seeks to serve. At the time of the 1870 Act, our modern world had not been invented – no cars or planes, no radio, TV, video and audio recording, no computers, internet, phones, digital cameras, etc. We do not know what the next half-century will bring, but we can be fairly confident that the changes will be at least as dramatic as those of the last 50 years

Clearly, it would not be possible to abolish existing institutions and systems overnight, but the value of a 'thought experiment' is that it will highlight the fundamental

1

issues which will need to be resolved to allow educational policy to be developed in a consistent and coherent way.

It would be unrealistic to expect thinking of this kind to emerge solely from the educational system itself, where people are fully engaged in making the present system work and dealing with all the immediate problems it throws up. Moreover, they are more likely to be prisoners of existing thinking and assumptions than those outside the system – new inventions often come from outside the industry they belong to (e.g. the Xerox copier, the Dyson washing machine – to name but a few). Not that individuals from education will be excluded in any way from the exercise – their perspective from first-hand experience, will be a particularly valuable contribution"

Ideally, we would have liked to publicise the project widely, possibly by running a national competition with substantial advertising support. However, SEI did not have the resources to do this and we had to be content with personal approaches to individuals we thought might be interested in contributing (including some well-known names in education). We also announced the project on the Internet

The response was encouraging: people, from the US, Australia, New Zealand and Singapore as well as the UK, expressed a willingness to contribute. Clearly, we had touched a nerve! We would like to express our thanks to the 21 authors whose chapters make up this book; they have all contributed voluntarily (no royalties will be paid to them or the editors) and have collaborated generously with our editorial demands. Any profits from this publication will be used to advance the work of SEI in promoting creativity and innovation in education.

We did not impose any editorial viewpoint on the content of the contributions – to do so would have been contrary to the spirit of the project. We accepted everything that in our opinion was relevant to the brief, intelligible to the general reader and within our length limits. We expressed our own ideas in our individual chapters

Neither have we attempted any synthesis of the contributions. It could not do justice to the wide variety of ideas and opinions expressed by our authors and it would be contrary to the purpose of the book, to be an open-minded exploration of a wide range of possibilities. We hope that it will stimulate the readers' own thinking and trigger fresh ideas. We see it as a start of an ongoing dialogue (not debate!); we suggest that the reader approaches the material in a non-judgmental frame of mind, not so much "do I agree with that" as "what else does that suggest" and "how might we make that happen". We hope to make a facility available on the SEI website www.excite-education.org for reader's comments and contributions

The book is not intended to be read through from beginning to end and there is no particular significance in the sequencing of the chapters. To assist the reader to find the chapters of greatest interest we have provided a Guide to the Contents, in which the authors provide a brief synopsis of their chapters.

Having had the privilege of absorbing the material ourselves over a period of time, we would like to share a couple of over-riding impressions. The first is the huge opportunity that exists for positive change arising from the confluence of the massive growth of technology, the results of research into the functioning of the brain and the growing understanding of the psychology of human development, particularly the critical importance of the Early Years experiences.

The second is the passionate commitment of so many people inside and outside the education system to finding ways to equip future generations to live successfully in whatever sort of world they find themselves growing up in, a world that will probably be as different from today's world as today's world is from those that we grew up in.

There are some encouraging signs of change already taking place; indeed one prospective contributor withdrew because he discovered that all the changes he had intended to propose were already happening in some part of the system! They include the establishment of an Innovation Unit in the Department for

Education, the Sure Start programme, the extension of school opening hours to provide breakfast clubs, homework clubs and study facilities and the proposals to transform early years work into a fully fledged profession, possibly on the lines of the Danish 'social pedagogue' model.

And therein lies a potential danger, that of putting new wines into old bottles. The education system is littered with brave and innovative pilot projects showing encouraging signs of success, which promptly die when the initial funding runs out, instead of being nurtured and incorporated into the mainstream. Like any large and old-established institution, the education system has its own 'Dynamic Conservatism' – the unconscious tendency to neutralise change while appearing to invite and welcome it (see Donald Schon, Beyond the Stable State, based on his 1970 Reith Lectures).

So long as mainstream education continues to be dominated by the narrow academic perspective of intellectual ability as manifested in exams, SATs etc., (A levels as the Gold Standard) and to be achieved by teaching in schools with compulsory attendance, valuable innovations are likely to die from lack of support. We need a radical shift in educational thinking; we hope this book will help to start a dialogue which can produce the necessary shift.

GUIDE TO THE CONTENTS – AUTHORS' SYNOPSES

potential.

Any forecast of the future is unlikely to get it right,
so it is hard to say what education system would be
appropriate for 50 years' time. That makes a vision
of what we would want to see all the more important.
Five principles to underpin the compulsory stages
of education are set out, starting from the need to
educate for uncertainty, which we can be sure will be
an issue. The practical implications of these principles
are then discussed. The adoption of a competence-
based system, where learning is integrated into
life, not separate from it, and where we seek to
develop reflective learners, is advocated. Piloting of a
competence-based curriculum has demonstrated its
ability to meet future needs.

Currently, verbal communication plays only a
secondary role in our approach to education; a poor
relation to the 'real work' of reading and writing.
Overwhelmingly, we use written means to teach,
test and evaluate our children. Written work is what
parents and school inspectors always demand to see
The underlying assumption, which is firmly rooted in
the minds of many pupils, parents and teachers, is
that talking is trivial and that being 'good at talking'
is a refinement rather than a basic requirement.
It is as if speaking and listening are peripheral in
comparison to reading and writing. This seems to be
completely the wrong way around. A proficiency in
spoken communication, i.e. dialogue, is the foundation
for literacy, but a proficiency in reading and writing
is no guarantee at all of effective interpersonal

communication. The cart has ended up leading the horse.

61 Stranger than Fiction
Barry Fryer, senior associate the Creativity Centre Ltd., designer of innovative learning materials, former Professor, Leeds Metropolitan University

The future of education is hard to predict. However, we can reasonably expect that it will be inextricably linked to the knowledge economy. Powerful direct interaction between learning materials and the human brain will probably be developed. Acquiring knowledge will become easier and more interesting. But there will be fresh problems, such as maintaining students' social skills in an age of individuality. We are already seeing an erosion of social life, as we spend progressively more time embroiled in information technology. We will need to find new ways to manage the learning of social skills and attitudes, leading to coherent benefits for individuals and society. We may need mentors to take the place of teachers. We may need to replace classrooms with highly interactive, super-PCs; with flexible, less structured social interaction in various venues. One vision of future education is that it may not lie in teaching facts; these may be largely self-taught. It may focus on inspiring students to develop skills and behaviour for creating a more integrated, tolerant society, where personal growth is viewed not in selfish terms, but in terms of the common good.

71 An Enterprising Education
Gerard Darby, researcher, writer and trainer, specialising in enterprise, creativity and lateral thinking

We need a much more enterprising approach to education. One which:
- recognises that failure is an important aspect of learning

- appreciates that there needs to be a switch of emphasis away from knowledge to know-how
- breaks down the boundaries between subject areas, between formal and informal learning and between the teacher and the student.

Successful learning puts the student at the core of education and values the diversity in different learning styles, different ideas and different behaviours. Enterprise skills are lifeskills and can be valuable to everyone whether working for themselves, for other people or in public service

83   Embodied Choices and Voices

Penelope Best (senior arts therapies clinician, trainer and supervisor)

A poetic call for the physical body experience to be more central in education, in learning experiences, especially at a time of changing environments and technological innovation.

93   Village Soup – Some Old Ideas Mixed Differently

John Alexander (businessman, former creativity and innovation consultant)

Based on ideas and conversations with teachers, parents and friends, all of whom felt strongly about education, and a brief report from some users - kids in school who seemed not to care and were interested in everything that did not include their school or their teachers, I have distilled six concepts:
- The involvement and education of parents
- Changing the way teachers are paid
- Developing a 'virtual one-room schoolhouse'
- Creating Local Learning Centres
- Pay teenagers for Civic Service before entering Higher Education
- Using retired people in education.

Gill Hope, Senior Lecturer in Design and Technology Education, KentTechnology Dept., University of Kent

Technology education is vital for children growing up in an age that is increasingly technology-dependent. However, if this is equated with vocational training, then we are providing an education bounded in a world-view that is being superceded by new realities. It is through the empowerment of making creative and responsible design choices that children are enabled to make sense and contribute towards the ever-changing world that will become tomorrow.

Marilyn Fryer and Caroline Fryer Director, Creativity Centre, Halifax and Chief Executive, The Creativity Centre Educational Trust

Unlike technological and social change which occur swiftly, human development changes on an evolutionary timescale. So, the challenge for the future is how to create appealing and effective educational provision that takes account of people's intellectual, social, emotional and physical development in what are certain to be very different technological and social contexts.

Historically, UK education has focused primarily on intellectual development at the expense of other aspects. This imbalance needs to be redressed and, in order to equip people both for the present and the future, developing creativity needs to be high on the educational agenda. This chapter looks at the broad implications for current and future education; and outlines some proposals for creating flexible, high quality and motivating learning environments.

In this chapter the Steiner (Waldorf) approach to child
education is presented as the most comprehensively
holistic educational vision and praxis ever devised
– one that carries the promise of healing the atomising
reductionism and nihilism of modern materialistic
education systems that typify Late Modernity. Three
broad themes are briefly explored: modernity's assault
on the very being of the child; the problem of State
incursion into, and control of, children's education;
and the role of child education in the progressive
evolution of human consciousness. It is argued that
only an educational ethos and milieu which strives
to transcend the crass utilitarianism and soulless
aridity of a one-sidedly materialistic education system
will serve to advance the healthy evolution of human
civilisation

A wish for education to embrace a paradigm shift,
expressed through an imaginary excursion to a
history class in my ideal fantasy school, where
classes are modelled on the processes developed by
MIECAT (Melbourne Institute of Experiential Creative
Art Therapy). The advantages and applications of
embodied creativity (integrating the sensing body
into the creative equation) are explored. I have given
examples of experiential, creative, embodying, teaching
practices drawn from my adult group singing classes,
and creative process classes. Also an example of an
experimental adaptation of these methods to remedial

This short chapter summarises conclusions from a mass of research evidence on cognition and schooling, particularly in the Early Years and in pupils' experiences and opinions. The principles derived from the empirical research stress the damage done by schools, the impossible position of teachers and the mistaken curriculum. Instead we note the desire for a far earlier, richer input and support of parents and the community and the involvement of people outside the system. The need to understand and act on the research evidence is stressed so that children's needs are met and the problems of society understood. Pupils' views of their ideals and hopes are summarised.

The key requirement of any education system is to nurture the child's connection-making confidence and ability, particularly by avoiding negative feedback which the child experiences as punishing rather than loving. Parents, family and teachers need to encourage approximate connections and the risk-taking courage that underlies them. The chapter explores the origins of this sensitivity in early childhood, using data from current brain research, the insights of psychologists in the 50s and 60s and the experience derived from videotaping working groups in business to find ways to enhance their creativity

of thinking about and solving learning and curricula problems. Two examples of the inclusion of brain concepts in education are given; one for language education and the other for mathematics.

Christopher Gilmore, teacher of self-development skills to children, actor and writer of Playshops and guidebooks to stimulate creativity

Constant accountability at all levels of education can anaesthetise personal initiatives and creativity. The author, who has taught all ages, proposes a complementary approach to amplify the less person-centred aspects of government directives. Using the model of a healthy diet, emphasis here is placed on the inner learner; all students, even from the youngest years, being encouraged into self-management through the holistic nourishment of their personal gifts. A happy childhood can last a lifetime. So whole-person health and happiness is the greatest gift, for without it, no success will be sustained. The approach encourages us all to feel special by knowing we can find in ourselves the best answers to our own best questions.

Gary Boyd Professor Education (Educational Technology Doctoral Programme) Concordia University, Canada

We need to generate understanding of the complex systems we are in, and that are in us. Particularly these should be designed to educate our critical capacities and so immunise against the various sorts of manipulation of public opinion now so widely practised through the mass media. Five factors are essential for re-inventing education for realistic hope: - Creative imagination, Scientific understanding, Technical capability, discursive political legitimacy, and far-sighted love. The tools will include IT and satellite-broadcast supported drama, simulations, and learning conversations

There are fetishes and taboos in education. Literacy and numeracy are the two most notable - these skills have been made obsolete by computer software over the past quarter century. They say our brains will rot if we can't do sums in our heads and spell correctly. And, programming is bad for children (because teachers don't understand it.)

Change in education over the past has been driven by short term political considerations and as a result has often been hasty and ill-considered. Much that was valuable has been destroyed in the attempt to correct perceived deficiencies. The author gives numerous examples and proposes the creation of an Education Policy Committee (analogous to the Bank of England's Monetary Policy Committee). Its remit would be to ensure that proposed changes are evidence-based, independently evaluated and have the support of the professionals whose commitment is essential to their success.

THE ORGANISED ENCOURAGEMENT OF LEARNING

Vincent Nolan

When I first got involved with Education, in 1985, a Principal Educational Psychologist I was working with characterised the present educational system as 'the organised discouragement of learning'. (And that was before the National Curriculum, Ofsted, SATS, numeracy and literacy hours etc.!)

The expression registered with me as the total antithesis of what I expect from education, namely The Organised Encouragement of Learning. How might we achieve that in the first half of this century, if we were unconstrained by existing institutions, systems, beliefs etc.?

Implicit in any proposals for future education is a vision of the kind of society we want to create. So I will make my vision explicit. I would like to see a society of people who are

- happy with their lives, confident with their ability to create the kind of life they want for themselves
- enjoying good relationships with their fellow human beings, whether partners, family, friends, neighbours, co-workers, competitors or society's representatives (such as police, tax inspectors and so on.
- in good health, physically, mentally and emotionally
- taking responsibility for themselves and their relationships, without blaming others for anything that goes wrong in their lives
- aware of their responsibilities to society (including people less fortunate than themselves) and the wider environment

They sound like a bunch of paragons! Yet I have faith that human beings are born with this potential (unless physically or mentally disabled in some way). It is the job of 'education' in the widest sense, to nurture the fulfilment of that potential, throughout the whole of a lifetime, by developing the capacity to learn continuously, by seeking out the knowledge they need and learning from their experiences

My Vision is not explicitly 'economic' in nature, though individuals who want to achieve a high level of material wealth will pursue it through economic means. It says nothing about the effect on Gross Domestic Product – for me, education is not about achieving national material goals (especially when measured by such a flawed instrument as GDP!) but about enabling people to fulfil their potential in whatever way they choose

Since the future is 'stubbornly unknowable', as John Naughton (1) puts it, we need to follow the principles established by Tim Berners-Lee for the Internet: no central ownership or control, keep the system as simple as possible by specifying only the ends, leaving it to the users to work out the detail of how to get what they want from it. I have attempted to suggest how education should begin and what end-point it should aim at

The nature of the Learning Process

I have no specialist knowledge in this field, but from my own experience and observation (particularly of my 13 grandchildren) I am convinced that learning is a natural and enjoyable process, provided that the individual is allowed to learn what and how and when they wish. It can be forced, as it has been in the past, by fear, backed up by corporal punishment, but the side effects far outweigh any conceivable benefits

It is also an individual process – different people learn in different ways; they are motivated to learn different things at different times, according to their own current interests. If this is the case, it cannot make sense as a 'mass market', with everyone learning the same things in groups (classes) at the same time. Today, the availability of the Internet creates the possibility of obtaining all the information you want when you want it. What is needed is the skills of accessing the Internet and the critical ability to assess the quality of what is on offer. As with any other skills, they are developed by practice and coaching (to guide the practice and ensure that lessons are learned from it)

Many skills can only be learned by practice in group situations – interpersonal and communication skills, teamwork, arts like drama and ensemble music, team sports etc. So facilities and coaching must be available for those who want to engage, voluntarily, in activities of this kind, not only children but adults also (learning is a lifelong activity)

Responsibility for Learning

Responsibility for learning, it seems to me, is shared by three parties – the individual 'student', parents and society (whether represented by the state or a more localised authority). The adult 'student' will be 100% responsible for their own learning; they may well look for help and guidance from others, particularly parents and also society, but the responsibility remains firmly with the student. For the most part, the adult should expect to pay for the help he/she seeks

Equally, the infant cannot be responsible for their own learning in the same conscious way as the adult (though they are still the person doing the learning). Here the responsibility must be first and foremost with the parents, to provide the secure emotional environment that is essential to allow the child's natural learning abilities to unfold. Recent brain research has highlighted the enormous importance of earliest experiences for the development of synapses in the brain – see for example Why Love Matters: How Affection Shapes a Baby's Brain, by Sue Gerhardt (2). The implication for education is that the priority has to be the emotional development of babies to lay a good foundation for future learning. Training in parenting skills and childcare would seem to be a priority. The parents are also responsible for providing access to learning opportunities and materials – toys, books, singing and dancing classes, etc.

The role of society is to support the parents in this vital

work and monitor, through the child's development, that it is succeeding. If not, society must provide remedial resources. I propose the appointment of a mentor for every child and its parents from the birth of the child. Initially the mentor would act as a coach in parenting skills – given that being a parent is the most important work any of us undertake in our lifetime, it is essential that we have the opportunity to learn the skills, under trained guidance, at the time we most need them

As the child grows, the mentor would increasingly focus on building a relationship with the child and suggesting to the parents ways in which the child's learning might be enhanced. The mentor would be essentially a 'friend of the family'. Once the child has acquired the core learning competencies, they are in a position to take increasing responsibility for their own learning

Society's role would be to supply the mentors (trained to a suitable quality level) and the learning resources, plus a safety net for any child who was failing to reach an adequate level of competence

Although it is natural for healthy children in stable environments to learn the essential learning skills, not all children will grow up in the appropriate conditions – absence of parents, poverty and deprivation of all kinds, physical and mental handicaps may hinder the natural learning and development process

Society has a responsibility to ensure that *every* child has acquired the core competencies and will need an assessment at some point to check whether this has been achieved. So society needs formally to check, at an appropriate age (whatever age that may be) that the child has developed the core learning skills to enable them to pursue their learning through later childhood and beyond

The assessment process need not be burdensome for the child or assessor; it might need no more than a certificate from the child's mentor that the appropriate level had been reached, with a sample of each mentor's assessments being audited independently. The assessment could well include a health check on the child's physical development. For children who are not reaching the required standard, remedial programmes would have been designed earlier by the mentor; if they had not been effective, an element of compulsion could come in. In the extreme, Society already has the power ultimately to take a child away from its parents and into 'care'

The Core Learning Skills

Conventionally, the core learning skills are described as the 3 R's – reading, writing and 'rithmetic; more grandly, literacy and numeracy. But the original 3 Rs were significantly different: apparently, the "phrase was a misquotation of an earlier aphorism - reading and writing, reckoning and figuring, wroughting and wrighting

"From reading and writing we get LITERACY, from reckoning and figuring comes NUMERACY. But we have no equivalent term for wroughting and wrighting - the creation and making of things"(3). I would add that 'reckoning and figuring' is a much broader concept than mere arithmetic or even numeracy

The shift is a symptom of the hi-jacking of education by the academics, which Professor Graham Sills (4) describes as the "vanquishing of substance by intellect" as a result of which "Britain remains a clever nation but woefully incompetent". Our present education system seems to be designed by scholars to produce more scholars. Scholars are valuable people – so too are plumbers, electricians, doctors, nurses, computer programmers etc. The values of scholarship are appropriate only to those who wish to become scholars or pursue 'scholarly' careers, e.g. research scientist. They are not necessarily suitable for everyone and should not be imposed on them

The old version of the 3R's (Reading and Reckoning, Wroughting and Wrighting), though an improvement on Reading, Writing and 'Rithmetic, needs to be modified to meet the needs and opportunities of the 21st century. I suggest:

- Communication (of which reading and writing are subsets) to allow for the inclusion of oral communication skills – speaking and listening, especially listening. It may be thought that because children normally come to school able to communicate orally, nothing further needs to be done. On the contrary – modern research demonstrates that everyday communication is seriously flawed, giving rise to many misunderstandings and interpersonal conflicts.
- Thinking Skills, to include creative as well as analytical thinking (reckoning and numeracy)
- Practical Skills, the old Wroughting and Wrighting updated to suit modern conditions and modern technology. I am not equipped to suggest what these skills should be, but they should generate a confidence to deal with manual problems and opportunities as they arise, whether in the home, car, computers, cameras, phones etc
- a whole new area of competence, Information and Communications Technology, particularly the ability to access the Internet. This skill could largely replace the traditional learning and memorising of factual information. Similarly, skill in the use of calculators could replace much of the manipulative skills of traditional mathematics (but not the thinking skills and the understanding of the mathematical concepts)

Once the core learning skills have been mastered, the child will move into a second phase, during which the child/student increasingly takes responsibility for their own learning. There would still be an individual mentor, but the relationship would be more directly between mentor and student (with the parents as supportive observers) and would focus on guiding the student to the resources that will help them pursue their own learning interests

As well as providing the mentors, society will want to be satisfied that, as the child approaches adulthood, they are equipped to take on the rights and responsibilities of an adult. If certain core competencies are deemed to be essential to function effectively in society, how do we establish that young people reaching adulthood have acquired them? In fact, we already know how to do this, for particular competencies that are needed for particular purposes. The driving test to obtain a driving licence provides an excellent model – it is accepted as a necessity and people choose to take driving lessons (at paid for schools or from friends and relatives). They also pay to take the test as often as necessary to gain the qualification. Furthermore, society can take the licence away as a punishment for serious driving offences or an accumulation of lesser offences (penalty points). Taking the test is not in itself compulsory – unless you want to drive

Suppose we were to adopt similar principles of voluntary learning for a required qualification for a general Certificate of Personal Maturity (a less pompous title would be preferable). The Certificate would be a prior condition to obtaining a passport, driving license, credit, the right to buy tobacco and alcohol (which we currently decide simply on age). Most employers would probably demand one as a condition of employment. There would be strong motivation to obtain the certificate. If it were subject to endorsement or suspension for criminal offences, anti-social behaviour, binge-drinking etc., it would also act as a powerful deterrent to crime

The assessment process would be wide-ranging; it would include a medical examination, physical exercises (e.g. running, swimming, climbing) and group exercises to assess interpersonal skills. The assessment would probably be residential and last a few days. Businesses, the armed services and the public services have plenty of experience of designing and running assessment programmes of this kind

In addition to the Learning Competencies required of the child (updated as appropriate for a young adult), other core competencies might be:

- Life Skills, including physical and mental health. As they reach maturity, people need to be equipped with the knowledge to make informed choices about their life style, including diet, exercise, smoking, drinking, drugs etc. Sex education would be a major topic, including its emotional as well as physical dimension. Awareness of the responsibilities of parenting would also be a part of it

- Interpersonal Skills and Emotional Intelligence. Ideally, people would be equipped to take responsibility for their own lives, including their feelings. They need to be aware of their emotions and able to manage them, so they can interact constructively with their families, friends and colleagues both at work and in their leisure activities. Ability to work in teams would be a component of this

The list is illustrative rather than definitive, but it sketches a very different kind of education from that involved in obtaining A levels at high grades (reputedly the 'gold standard' of the present system). If the universities need A levels to help them select their intake, let them organise the tests they need and administer them as they see fit. Nothing is gained by making such tests, or university degrees, a general requirement of an educated person

The implications for 'education'

If the Certificate of Personal Maturity were the ultimate goal of the formal (pre-university) education process, the role of education would be to foster the development of the appropriate abilities and provide the facilities and coaching needed to achieve them. Compulsory attendance would have no part to play, except perhaps in remedial cases. Motivation on the part of the students would not be a problem – the importance of obtaining the Certificate would be obvious to them

Compulsory attendance at school would become a thing of the past. In fact, it is not a legal requirement even today. The obligation on parents is to ensure that their children are 'educated'. In practice, parents are faced with a binary choice – Home Education or enrolment in a school with compulsory attendance. I see no reason why we should not be able to have the best of both worlds. 'Schools' would become Learning Centres with voluntary attendance

Certainly we will need skilled people to guide and mentor the learning process; we also need facilities, both for group activities of the kind listed above and for individual learning – computer terminals connected to the Internet, libraries and quiet working places for those who cannot find them at home

But we do not need compulsory attendance for everyone at specified hours in certain weeks of the year, or the grouping of those who do attend in classes to be managed and instructed by a teacher. The Local Learning Centres would provide a base for the mentors who are responsible for assisting and monitoring the learning progress of the pupils assigned to them. Contact would be maintained directly between tutor and pupil (and their parents) using phones, e-mail and *occasional* face to face meetings as necessary. Part of the tutor's role would be to make the pupils aware of the learning facilities available and encourage them to participate in the group activities

I see the Learning Centres being open all year round (with occasional closure for maintenance) and all day into the evening. Mentors would take their holidays when they chose (as with most trades and professions); so would families. School holidays, school buses and the daily school run would become a thing of the past, as would the academic year (still geared to an agricultural society that no longer exists)

Many of the social problems encountered in a school environment (such as theft, bullying and anti-social behaviour) might be less likely to arise in an institution attended voluntarily by motivated students, than in today's schools (though the problems might only be transferred to other arenas). Teachers, in their new role as tutors/coaches would be free of the stress of classroom management and maintaining discipline. It is an attractive prospect, though one which might require retraining of many existing teachers

It must be acknowledged that the abolition of compulsory attendance at school could cause a problem for parents who expect the school to provide childcare while they go to work. The Learning Centres could have an acknowledged role as safe places for children and should probably charge for this 'child-minding' service. It would fit naturally with the provision of group activities – sport, drama, music, arts and crafts etc.- and learning facilities

Society may take fright at the prospect of gangs of marauding teenagers and sub-teenagers roaming the city streets, but if the learning centres were sufficiently attractive places, the students might prefer to be there (especially if a record of misbehaviour made the Maturity Certificate more difficult to obtain!). Some parents may well decide to spend more time with their children and less at work, if the child-minding provided by existing compulsory schooling was no longer free

Conclusion

I believe that if we could organise education on these principles, which try to clarify how responsibility divides between student, parents and society at different stages of development, we would have a radically different, and healthier situation than we have at present. I have not attempted to think through the economics of what I am proposing, but I suspect we would be able to dispense with a great deal of bureaucracy, quangos and institutions designed for a world we no longer live in. These savings might well offset the extra costs arising from the universal mentoring and more demanding assessment system for the Personal Maturity Certificate

At the moment, it does not make sense to blame schools, teachers or the education system for the many ills of our society, such as crime, anti-social behaviour, sexually transmitted diseases, obesity, drug and alcohol addiction etc; education is simply not designed to deal with such matters. In my scenario, however, it would make sense to judge the success or otherwise of 'education' by the prevalence or absence of such problems. A healthier society is a goal well worth pursuing

Vincent Nolan was Chairman of Synectics Ltd., the European division of the international creativity and innovation consultancy. He introduced the techniques into the UK in 1971. Since retiring from business, he has focused on introducing business creativity methods into education, through the Registered Charity, Synectics Education Initiative. He is the author of Open to Change (1984, MCB Publications), The Innovators Handbook (1989, Sphere Books) and editor of Creative Education (2000, Synectics Education Initiative)

References

(1) John Naughton: "Labour's love lost on the net" Observer, May 15 2005
(2) Sue Gerhardt: Why Love Matters
(3) Alan Fletcher, The Art of Looking Sideways, 2001, Phaidon Press
(4) Prof. Graham Sills, RSA Journal, Nov. 2004

LEARNING TO LEARN

Susie Parsons, former Chief Executive, Campaign for Learning

What's the point of education? At the most basic level, we educate children to be able to survive into adulthood, to earn a living, to meet their needs for food and shelter and to find their way around in the world without succumbing to the perils of junk food, obesity, drink or drugs. It's not just about survival, though. At best, we want people to flourish, to enjoy both intellectual stimulation and physical exercise, to take delight in scientific discovery, to appreciate and contribute to the wonderful range of art, music and literature with which we are surrounded, to have a rich emotional life and manage well our relationships with other human beings and to take care of our planet and its resources.

If education is about helping people to survive and flourish and realise their full potential, it needs to take account of the fact that we live in an uncertain world where we don't know today what we will need to learn in the future. The frontiers of human knowledge continue to expand and it is much less important to be able to hold information in one's head than to know where to find it and how to interpret it. The Internet gives us ready access to a mass of undifferentiated information so everyone needs to be able to select, evaluate and process information and discard what is not needed or helpful.

Today, people are less likely to stay in the same job for life. They may change jobs within an industry or move between industries and sectors. Even if they do stay in the same organisation, jobs and roles can change dramatically during a working life. Britain is no longer predominantly a manufacturing economy but increasingly a service and knowledge-based economy. In the past, a large number of jobs didn't even require basic literacy skills whilst today the vast majority involve intermediate or advanced level skills and the Director-General of the CBI, Digby Jones, predicts that in a few years time anyone who is without a skill will be without a job. Many children and young people who are at school now will grow up to do jobs which have not yet been invented. Their education needs to equip them to deal confidently with change.

Technological advances are rapid. When my grandmother was growing up in rural Wiltshire at the beginning of the last century, dip pens were just taking over from slates in schools. When I first started teaching in the early 1970s, we used Banda machines to make our own worksheets, fuelled with purple ink that stained your hands. Nowadays, we all take photocopiers, computers and mobile telephones for granted – but our current technology will seem laughably primitive to our grandchildren. Computer science, media studies, design and technology and a host of new subjects which were not on offer in the 1970s, have made their way into the school curriculum.

Since we don't know now what people will need to learn in the future, it makes perfect sense to develop confident, successful lifelong learners who are ready to learn anything. What John Holt wrote in the last century is just as true for this one: *Since we cannot know what knowledge will be most needed in the future, it is senseless to try to teach it in advance. Instead, we should try to turn out people who love learning so much and learn so well that they will be able to learn whatever needs to be learned.* (1)

Learning is a process of active engagement which enables us to make sense of the world, increases skills, knowledge and understanding and leads to change, development and the desire to learn more. The good news is that we are all born learners, programmed to learn from the outset. You only have to watch a baby exploring the world through touch and taste and imitation to see that - while a four-year old can ask up to 400 'why?' questions a day. Many people talk of lifelong learning as what happens to some of us after we leave compulsory education at the age of 16. In fact, of course, lifelong learning means just that – learning from cradle to grave.

As babies, we learn to walk and talk and explore the world without really being aware that we are learning.

Once we get into the formal education system, we start being taught things like reading, writing and using numbers, often with an emphasis on <u>what</u> we are learning rather than <u>how</u> we learn. The main function of formal education should be to help people to learn – to give them the motivation and ability to be confident successful learners as well as focusing on the content of their learning. This is not to suggest that content is unimportant, quite the contrary. Content and process are inextricably linked. You cannot develop thinking skills without something interesting to think about.

How can we make sure that people retain their curiosity, continue to grow their learning power and flourish as lifelong learners? We can teach them how to learn.

The Campaign for Learning is an independent charity which aims to stimulate learning that will sustain people for life. It focuses on three main areas: learning at work, family and community learning and learning in school. It runs national awareness-raising events, including Learning at Work Day and Family Learning Week, and works in a range of ways to change policy and practice on learning. The Campaign is working for an inclusive society in which learning is understood, valued and accessible to everyone as of right. Much of its activity in workplaces and in families and communities is directed towards helping people who are disengaged from learning to switch back on.

The work in schools, however, aims to assist teachers to make sure that their pupils and students stay switched on – building on the enthusiasm for learning which everyone is born with and which is evident to anyone watching a small child exploring the world. The rationale for the Campaign's Learning to Learn in Schools project is to understand how to help pupils and students to learn most effectively and so give each one the best chance to achieve his or her full potential. In practice, this has entailed investigation of a range of interventions aimed at recognising and supporting pupils' different learning styles and at making the learning process more explicit so as to develop independent learning skills and boost motivation. The project also investigates the impact of learning how to learn on pupil attainment and on teacher morale.

Starting in September 2000, phases 1 and 2 of the project involved teachers in 24 schools with pupils and students aged from three to 16 years old in action research. The results (2) from the first two years suggested that learning to learn can help to raise standards of attainment, enhance teacher morale and make schools more effective, inclusive and motivating for a wider range of pupils. Encouraged by these very positive results, the Campaign is now co-ordinating a larger research project (phase 3) for three years from September 2003, working with about 100 teachers and some 3,000 pupils in 32 primary and secondary schools in Cornwall, Cheshire and the London Borough of Enfield. The Centre for Teaching and Learning at the University of Newcastle upon Tyne is evaluating phase 3 and providing action research support to the project schools.

The report from Newcastle (3) on the first year of phase 3 and the action research investigations overwhelmingly show positive benefits for the pupils, teachers and schools taking part in the project. All of the schools report that learning to learn has had a positive impact on teaching and learning. Eighteen of the 31 case studies show a measurable impact on pupils' attainment although the effect on attainment will not really show up fully until the end of phase 3, particularly as many of the schools chose to concentrate on the pupils who will be sitting SATs or GCSEs in the last year of the project.

Developing knowledge and awareness of the pupil's or student's own learning is a key feature and case studies frequently also mention outcomes such as increased enthusiasm, motivation and happiness in school. There is evidence of impact on the teachers in terms of their own professional learning, improvement in motivation, confidence in using learning to learn strategies and approaches and increased belief and confidence in the success of these strategies to improve attainment and to help pupils see themselves as successful learners. Some of the schools involved parents in their activities and they have reported that parents found benefits for their own learning and development as well as their children's. Pupils and students appreciated having better understanding at home of what they do at school.

Interestingly, many of the schools which started small with just one or a few classes involved are now rolling-out learning to learn throughout the school. Some of the schools had an OFSTED inspection during the first year and received favourable comments on the quality of teaching and learning.

Throughout the project, the Campaign has worked with the participant schools to develop thinking on what learning to learn involves. From the beginning, it has drawn on a wealth of thinking and practice from a range of different disciplines. The theory and research sources underpinning learning to learn include cognitive psychology, neuroscience, theories of learning and intelligence, work on formative assessment and thinking skills, motivational psychology, emotional intelligence, learning environments, health and nutrition. These various theories and approaches have been used to develop a single model of learning to learn - the 5Rs for lifelong learning. While taking full responsibility for this model, the Campaign acknowledges with gratitude the work of Guy Claxton, Bill Lucas, Alistair Smith and Toby Greany on which it is based.

The 5Rs are as follows:
- **Readiness:** learners know how to assess their own motivation, to set goals, to achieve a positive learning state, including their preferred learning environment and to talk about learning.
- **Resourcefulness:** learners know how the mind works and humans learn, to assess their own preferred learning style, to seek out and use information, including through ICT, to communicate effectively in different ways and to use various approaches to learning.
- **Resilience:** learners know how to apply learned optimism, to empathise and use emotional intelligence, to proceed when stuck and to ask critical questions.
- **Remembering:** learners know how to use various memory techniques, to make connections and to apply learning in

different contexts.

- **Reflectiveness:** learners know how to ask questions, observe, see patterns, experiment and evaluate their learning.

The table, from *Creating a Learning to Learn School* (4), shows the attitudes, attributes, skills and knowledge which education needs to help people to develop if they are to become confident successful lifelong learners.

	Attitudes/Attributes	**Skills** Demonstrates ability to:	**Knowledge** Knows how:
Readiness	Motivation Curiosity Self-belief/esteem Self-efficacy (optimism re the learning outcome, confidence and willingness to take risks)	Assess and manage own motivation towards a task Set specific goals which connect to particular learning Achieve a positive learning state Manage own learning process Talk about learning to learn in relation to a new task	To assess own motivation To set goals and connect to the learning To use a Learning to Learn language To assess own preferred learning environment
Resourcefulness	Learning from and with others Learning creatively in different ways Flexibility	Make most of preferred learning style and environment Develop and expand learning repertoire and to harness creativity Find and use information Communicate effectively in different ways	The mind works and how humans learn To assess own preferred learning style and environment To use different approaches to learning To seek out and use information, including through ICT To communicate effectively in different ways
Resilience	Keeping going Learning under stress Managing feelings about learning and teachers, peers and resources	Persist and apply learned optimism and self-belief/self-efficacy approaches empathise and use Emotional Intelligence Use different approaches when stuck	To use learned optimism and self-efficacy approaches To empathise and use EQ approaches To proceed when stuck
Remembering	Maximising own memory Applying learning Practising	Use different memory approaches Make connections Apply learning/use what has been learned, including in different contexts	To use different memory approaches To make connections To apply learning, including in different contexts
Reflectiveness	Looking back Improving learning and performance	Stop and reflect (e.g. ask questions, observe, see patterns) Experiment with learning Evaluate learning	To stop and reflect (e.g. ask questions, observe, see patterns). To experiment with learning To use different ways to evaluate

The teachers, students, pupils and parents who are taking part in the Learning to Learn in Schools project are demonstrating that a great deal can be done within the existing education system to produce confident, successful lifelong learners, but how can we change the system to make it easier for them and increase their chances of success? What would an education system based on the interlocking propositions of developing lifelong learners and teaching people how to learn look and feel? I do not have a complete blueprint but I think that there are a number of key features.

Clarity about the purpose of education

I have argued in this chapter that the purpose of education is to teach people how to become confident, successful, lifelong learners who are able to learn anything they need to learn in the future. This needs to be explicitly recognised within the education system. From pre-school, through school, further and higher education, work-based learning, adult and community learning and family learning provision, the focus needs to be on developing the 5Rs.

'Teachers' and 'learners'

We need to get away from the notion of the teacher as the guardian of a body of knowledge to be imparted to and passively absorbed by the learner. As Guy Claxton has said 'Helping young people become better learners may mean daring to give up the belief that a teacher's top responsibility is to be omniscient.' (5) We need to promote the idea that what successful teachers do is to model learning themselves, build the learning power of others and encourage collaborative learning; one of the best ways to learn something oneself is to teach it to someone else. The role of the teacher as learning coach and recognition that the teacher is also a learner needs to be embedded in our approach to pedagogy and in both initial teacher training and continuous professional development.

Educational institutions and the 'real world'
We need to create coherence between what happens inside

and what happens outside our educational establishments. Learning should be a normal part of everyday experience in families, communities and workplaces not just something that happens in special places called schools, colleges and universities. We should also make better use of these special places and the resources which they contain. Rather than lying empty for much of the time, educational institutions should be opened up as community learning centres. Kate Myers has floated the idea of 24 hour schools. 'One version of the 24-hour school that would be possible to introduce now would be for young people of compulsory school age to have priority access to the facilities between 9-4 with the school open to the community the rest of the time'. (6)

We need to design and organise our educational institutions in such a way as to promote learning, by:

- taking full advantage of ICT including access to specialist teachers and resources and the ability for students to work from home;
- providing facilities for group, paired and individual learning;
- designing creative learning zones;
- enabling students to work in depth on a particular project rather than stopping after 40 minutes and moving on to an unconnected subject;
- sending students out to learn in venues such as museums and workplaces.

Curriculum

Should learning to learn be a separate subject in its own right or should it be embedded throughout the curriculum or parts of the curriculum? During the first two phases of our Learning to Learn project, several schools evaluated the impact of providing 'learning to learn' induction courses or timetabled lessons; others explored the application of thinking skills and learning to learn approaches in specific subject areas; others investigated developing a wider school culture to support learning to learn. Some of the different methods used in phase 3 include the following:

- Two primary schools have incorporated their learning to learn approach into specified days when the usual curriculum is suspended and the focus is solely on learning to learn.
- A primary school has implemented learning to learn in PE and found that the pupils enjoy the lessons and take away the learning to learn techniques and use them in other lessons.
- A secondary school is assessing the impact of a whole school learning to learn strategy.
- A number of primary and secondary schools have taken a more generalised approach and used multiple learning to learn strategies in the classroom to underpin teaching and learning.

Both dedicated learning to learn classes and embedding learning to learn in the classroom seem to lead to positive results, so it seems sensible to use both approaches.

Assessment for learning and qualifications

Formative assessment, developed by Paul Black and Dylan Wiliam (7), is being used successfully in many of our project schools. This involves assessment for rather than of learning – that is, information being fed back to the learner by the teacher to be used by the learner to make improvements. This does not mean rejecting summative assessment – assessment of learning - or national tests and standards. Learners have a right to know how they are doing and to gain qualifications and parents have a right to know how their children are getting on at school. As David Hargreaves has said 'From the perspective of lifelong learning, however, it must be the improvement of learning that is the highest priority and while reporting on each student's attainment is important, *it must be done in a way that contributes to the improvement of teaching and learning.* (8)'. What is needed is both formative assessment and summative assessment linked to a modular qualifications system which is both comprehensive and comprehensible.

Personalised Learning

Finally, it is impossible to conceive of learning to learn without including the idea of personalised learning. Learning to learn approaches are, by definition, learner-centred. They aim to engender the optimal learning environment and learning support for all pupils and students and to make explicit the process of learning so that all pupils and students are able to reflect on the way that they learn and develop the skills and understanding that will make them confident, independent learners.

Susie Parsons' work experience spans the health service, local government and the voluntary and public sectors. A former Chief Executive of the Commission for Racial Equality, she now runs her own management consultancy specialising in strategic planning and review, leadership and change management, public relations and internal communication and quality, equality and diversity. Having begun her working life as a teacher of French in an inner-city school in London, Susie subsequently held the posts of Director of Community Education for Shelter, Housing Projects Officer at North Kensington Law Centre, Chief Officer for Paddington and North Kensington Community Health Council, General Manager of the London Energy and Employment Network and Head of Press, Publicity and Information for the London Borough of Hackney. She was appointed to the post of Executive Director of London Lighthouse in September 1994 and became its Chief Executive in January 1997. From 1999 to 2001 she was Chief Executive of the Commission for Racial Equality and subsequently worked as an independent management consultant for a range of national and local organisations. She became Chief Executive of the Campaign for Learning in June 2002 and left in May 2005, having fulfiled the three-year commitment which she made when she joined. She has written and edited publications on subjects ranging from education to energy efficiency, women in management and health and social care issues.

References

(1) John Holt *How Children Learn* Penguin 1965

(2) Toby Greany and Susie Parsons *Learning to Learn in Schools* Campaign for Learning 2004

(3) Steve Higgins, Kate Wall, Chris Falzon, Elaine Hall and David Leat *Learning to Learn in Schools Phase 3 Evaluation Year 1 Final Report* Campaign for Learning/University of Newcastle upon Tyne 2005

(4) Toby Greany and Jill Rodd *Creating a Learning to Learn School* Campaign for Learning/Network Educational Press 2003

(5) Guy Claxton *Learning to Learn: a key goal in a 21st century curriculum* Contribution to QCA Futures project 2005

(6) Kate Myers *Do we still need schools?* Contribution to QCA Futures project 2005

(7) Paul Black and Dylan Wiliam *Inside the Black Box - raising standards through classroom assessment* 1998

(8) David H. Hargreaves *Learning for Life – the foundations for lifelong learning* Lifelong Learning Foundation/Policy Press 2004

COMPETENCE-BASED EDUCATION

Valerie Bayliss

The problem with looking at what approach to education will meet the needs of society in half a century's time is the implication that we have some idea what that society will look like. Yet track records in predicting the future so far ahead are pretty poor. There are some assumptions we can make with reasonable confidence: technology will have moved a long way from where it is now, albeit in ways we can't foresee; life will be changing fast - it always does; human beings will still behave like human beings, with - thank goodness – all the magic and perversity that entails. Beyond that lies uncertainty.

This is no argument against setting out a vision - rather the contrary. One of the problems about education thinking in Britain is the paucity of explicit vision. The bland rhetoric of white and green papers has never been an adequate substitute. But vision matters, even if implicit, because it drives decisions. The other big problem is that fundamental change in education is slow, a process like turning a supertanker. This is partly to do with the sheer size of the system, though there are deeper factors at work. We underestimate at our peril the grip of history, culture and social attitudes on the way society and individuals think about education. The barriers to fundamental change are formidable. Yet at the most prosaic level, what is done to and in education now will have an impact on education in fifty years' time.

Against this background there is a good case for starting at the other end of the telescope. Let's think about what education might look like if we took the decisions that way. The starting point is a major rethink about what we believe young people's initial education is for. Motherhood and apple pie statements could flow too easily here. Everyone (more or less) wants well-adjusted, inquisitive young people with a strong sense of values, educated in a system which provides the opportunity to develop to the full every individual's particular talents and capacities. Such statements tell us everything and nothing. Better, I suggest, to proceed by setting out some principles from which the education system of the future - here, focusing on what we currently define as the compulsory stages of schooling - should develop. They are not novel. They are too often ignored.

First is the need to educate for uncertainty. If the world will change in ways we know not, a prime duty is to help individuals develop the capacity to live with the uncertainty and to flourish with it or in spite of it.

Second, comes the need to understand why the world is as it now is, and how it came to be. It is important to see this both as the context for learning and as central to the transmission of values and common culture between generations. On its own, however, it is not enough.

Third, we need to understand and make a reality of the notion that education as a process pervades all we do. Learning is not something that happens only in educational institutions.

Fourth, education needs to be based on respect: the mutual respect of teacher and learner, whoever and wherever the teachers and learners are.

Fifth, in education as in many other things, we shall do best if form follows function.

What does all this mean in practice?

Educating for uncertainty

This is not what most education systems have done in the past, but it would be fatal to ignore it in the future. It means turning present approaches to education on their heads. In my vision, the prime outcomes of initial education, what we want young people to take away from the process, are the competences they will need to manage and succeed in life - whatever life throws at them; not the acquisition of a specified quantum of information or knowledge about a given range of things (which might or might not be called 'subjects'). The latter has serious limitations, not least that it is essentially backward-looking and controlling rather than liberating. We have tried it, and seen the inadequacy of the results. Instead, we need a way to capitalise on the very factor that creates the problems. This will not happen by chance or as some welcome but unconsidered, unstructured by-product of the education process. Competence-based learning offers an answer.

That in turn implies an understanding of, and some consensus on, what competences – competence being defined as the ability to understand and to do - are needed. There is of course room for discussion, even controversy, about this, but perhaps not as much as appears at first blush. The Royal Society of Arts, Manufactures and Commerce (RSA) consulted widely a few years ago, among teachers and others, on what might go into a framework of competences that would serve as a statement of what initial education was offering young people, and as an organising principle for whatever curriculum was offered. Hundreds of suggestions were made; in discussion, there emerged much consensus on what should feature in an enduring framework.

Some years on, the framework has been tested by the RSA in a number of secondary schools as the basis for the organisation of teaching and learning for mainly 12 to 14 year olds. We know that it works; it has brought about real improvements in attainment, both in conventional testing and beyond, and in motivation and behaviour; it has energised teachers. In my vision, the national curriculum of the future will be a competence framework. The focus of assessment will be development of specific competences and only secondarily the acquisition of information - it would be more important to test the individual's ability to seek out and evaluate information and knowledge relevant to a particular issue.

Of course no framework of competences can be set in stone. Ideas and priorities change, both to reflect and to lead change in the world. The concept has an additional value as a focus for discussion on managing such changes. And the discussion can be real at a variety of levels: national, community, institutional, family, personal.

Understanding why and how the world is as it is

This is a crucial function of initial education. Young people cannot make much sense of life without a framework of information and knowledge. The problem is identifying what really needs to be covered in initial education. The amount of information on offer to them is already, thanks not least to technology, vastly bigger than it could be in the past, and than can be absorbed by any individual. In fifty years the volume will be unimaginable. Learners, and those who lead their learning, will struggle without a basic framework. At the same time, education has to be about more than what we already know. Understanding the why and how of change is equally important.

In my vision, the competence-based national curriculum of the future would be supported, but not led, by statements of the knowledge areas that should be covered; they would function as vehicles through which individuals' competences would be developed. And they would be starting points, not caps on the acquisition of knowledge; the system must allow for the individual of whatever age or stage who wants to delve deep into a particular area. Every statement would tell a child how and where to begin a search for further knowledge, through a variety of sources in the community, in the school, through technology. Experience of running a competence-based curriculum shows that it is sufficiently liberating of children's talents and imagination that they race ahead, covering more 'content' than the current national curriculum demands of them.

Education as a process pervades all we do

Young people learn in many ways and places. Everyone knows this but we have been very poor at capturing and recognising learning outside the formal education system. Perversely, education becomes defined as what goes on in educational institutions. In the future this will be even crazier than it is now. Well within fifty years, a mix of technology and increasingly personalised education programmes will make it feasible to recognise and capture learning that takes place outside the formal setting of schools. This has profound implications. It will become possible at last to abandon the damaging notion that education consists only of what is done at school, and match learner and learning environment effectively.

It is in the interest of every learner that there is a proper structure for managing this. The same competence framework can be used by leaders of learning in many settings: schools and teachers, parents and training providers. Crucially, it can be used by young learners themselves, for self- and peer-assessment and development. The framework becomes a shared tool. Young people would negotiate on how and where they would pursue their learning (and indeed its assessment). The statements of knowledge to be covered, discussed above, are relevant here. They would necessarily be broader than anything found in schools now. If you see content as a vehicle for learning it becomes possible to recognise the opportunities for learning in many more contexts than schools currently recognise.

Education must be based on mutual respect

The social relationships operating within schools are a major factor in determining the success or otherwise of young people's learning, and will always be so, even if school looks very different from today's model. The rhetoric about respect that features in a thousand school statements of values and ethos is daily belied by reality, on a number of levels. In an important sense, many teachers don't work 'with' young people; they work 'at' them. While it is not now the task of schools to remedy all of society's problems, they are not immune from them; this will not change. But a better framework for learning will go a long way to securing improvements.

A key issue here is how teachers see their role. It is much easier to teach than to promote and lead learning. Yet in an important sense, teaching never educated anyone; only learning does that. This is not a semantic question. Perhaps the most important finding to emerge from the RSA's experience to date in running a competence-based curriculum is that in every case, teachers have found it essential and highly effective to develop with their students a shared understanding of the purpose of what they are doing, and a shared sense of exploration. This has had a profound effect on the teacher-learner relationship and on the progress of students. This sharing is an important aspect of mutual respect. In my vision, it becomes an absolute requirement. There can be no place for the answer 'because you have to' to the question 'why must we do this?'. It follows, too, that there must be the same level of respect for all kinds of learning.

Teachers must become leaders of learning, rather than the sole fount of knowledge. The sheer expansion of information and knowledge in the world will make this shift more important, though that is not the main rationale for it. There are important implications here for the way teachers are trained. Education will still need subject experts, but they will need to be trained to work in a much broader context. They will need to develop expertise in using their subject knowledge in ways that support competence development and crucially to work in partnership with teachers across the range of subjects, co-ordinating the content that supports the curriculum in a way that rarely happens now. This has been done in the RSA's curriculum project; it works.

A second issue is who we see as leaders of learning. In my vision, more individuals, within and outside schools, will be recognised as such. Young people will respond positively, as they find leaders of learning more widely available in society, see their learning as pervading the whole of their lives and not as something confined to school, understand better what kind of things they may be able to learn in different settings and become active partners in designing and developing their education

Form follows function

The physical manifestation of initial education, the conventional school, has reigned supreme for centuries. Mostly it sits separate from civil society, a part of young people's life that bears little relationship to most of it. There are advantages in the conventional model. A crucial feature of education is socialisation, and schools provide excellent contexts for that (as well as an introduction to the rougher aspects of life, like bullying, whether by students or staff). They also support the efficient operation of the economy by safeguarding children while parents work. But should they still be such a dominant but self-contained feature in fifty years' time?.

The concept of an organisation that takes responsibility for organising young people's learning must and will remain central. It will need to have a physical location, in the middle of local communities. In its operation and composition it will be very different. In my vision, the school will negotiate the individual's learning programme, with individuals and their families. It will provide the physical location for some of the learning; but not all, for learning will be going on in a far wider range of settings: homes, libraries, museums, colleges, the countryside, other people's workplaces, through play. The school will negotiate access to these and will recognise a wide range of leaders of learning. It will supervise the recording systems that make a reality of individualised learning, and mediate assessment systems drawn from a variety of sources appropriate to the different forms of learning used by its students. Terms and school hours will be an irrelevance; if learning pervades life, the education system must adapt to recognise that. As it happens, a move away from shutting students out of schools for most of the time - which is what happens now - might even lead to their spending more time in them.

All this implies enormous changes in the way we think about and organise education. Radical change is hard to achieve in this aspect of life. Faced with a combination of uncertainty and cultural conservatism, can there be any confidence that a system incorporating this vision could be developed? Here, as at the start, we need to turn received views on their heads. We cannot afford not to go down this path. Whatever you think of traditional approaches to education – and they have had their value, in the past - they cannot serve us well in the future. Education cannot be immune from change, even though it occupies the almost unique role - so difficult to operate effectively - of having to mediate and explain the shift from past to future.

So, my vision is a learning system
- that starts from the individual, and holds that as a central principle;
- that recognises every individual as a learner, and that learning is an active concept;
- that is built round learners, developing their individual talents and capacities and reflecting the individual ways in which they can best learn;
- that makes the best use of technology and recognises what technology can't do;
- that dissolves the old barriers between schools and society, integrating education into life rather than separating it;
- that makes a reality of the relationship between learner and learning leader;
- that finds a way to transmit the values of society while educating the next generation for the future, not the past.

At root it is a vision for developing reflective learners, who understand their own ability to learn, who can find the opportunities for learning wherever they find themselves, who are well equipped to live in the world in which they find themselves. That will of course not be our world.

As it happens, the evidence exists that important elements of this vision, when put into practice, can work. It lies in the RSA's curriculum project, Opening Minds. For four years now, a number of schools have been using the RSA's competence framework to underpin and shape the learning of numbers of their students. They have done so with great success. The prospects for the whole vision are looking good. Opening Minds gives us a glimpse of the future, and shows us that it works.

Valerie Bayliss is an education consultant and former Director
of Education and Youth Policy at the Department of Employment.
She is the author of a number of reports published by the Royal
Society for the encouragement of Arts, Manufactures and Commerce
including Redefining Work (1998), Opening Minds (1999), and
Opening Minds: Taking Stock (2003).
Contact: via the RSA website http://www.thersa.org/
newcurriculum/

THE DIALOGUE DIVIDEND

Andrew Bailey

My vision: a primary school education system that is built on the principles and practices of dialogue.

Currently, verbal communication plays only a secondary role in our approach to education; a poor relation to the 'real work' of writing and reading. The primacy of literacy is deeply embedded in the culture of British school life. Overwhelmingly, we use written means to teach, test and evaluate our children. Written work is what parents and school inspectors always demand to see as evidence of achievement.

The underlying conclusion, which is firmly rooted in the minds of many pupils, parents and teachers, is that talking is trivial and that being 'good at talking' is a refinement rather than a basic requirement. One can only speculate about the impact that this daily message has on people's lifelong attitude towards interpersonal communication.

It is as if speaking and listening are peripheral in comparison to reading and writing. To me, this seems to be completely the wrong way around. A proficiency in spoken communication, i.e. **dialogue**, is the foundation for literacy, but a proficiency in reading and writing is no guarantee at all of effective interpersonal communication. The cart has ended up leading the horse.

Before I present you with the full logic of my argument, I need to explain in some detail what I mean by dialogue.

The Characteristics of Dialogue

In my definition, dialogue is a qualitatively distinct form of conversation. It is conversation at its most inclusive, productive and rewarding. Here is a checklist of some of the essential characteristics of dialogue.

The participants in a dialogue **share the airtime**. Both people get the opportunity to make their points. The conversation is **two-way**. If someone has a useful or important point to contribute, they're encouraged to make it.

In a dialogue, people communicate *with* each other rather than *at* each other. They **connect** and **interact** as people rather than make speeches. When Person A speaks, Person B listens, considers what he or she is hearing and often acknowledges the point that's been made. (And vice versa.) Not all conversations are like this. Many conversations are more like intersecting monologues than chains of interconnected remarks.

Because they are interactive, dialogues are essentially **spontaneous**. They cannot be rehearsed like the lines of a play.

In a dialogue, people **take full responsibility for being understood**. Person A takes responsibility for making sure his or her points are fully understood by Person B. (And vice versa.) It is self-defeating to blame the other person for not understanding you. In a dialogue, you check that you've been understood rather than assume it. You recognise that the act of communication is completed at the receiving end, not at the transmitter.

In a dialogue, people **take full responsibility for understanding the other person**. Person A takes responsibility for making sure he or she understands exactly what Person B is trying communicate, even if Person B is not being very clear, or is feeling angry or defensive. (And vice versa.) If you cannot understand the other person's point, it is counter-productive to blame them for not being able to express it well. Who's interests does that serve? In a dialogue, it is your job to help the other person be clear and complete, especially if they are finding it difficult to be articulate.

Taking responsibility for understanding someone's point of view involves tuning in, paying attention, listening on all channels (non-verbal as well as verbal), being aware of the other person's state of mind and mood, prompting and probing, demonstrating empathy, challenging inconsistencies, and so on. This set of skills is a far cry from the passive listening conventionally taught in schools. (Listening to someone read a story is a very different task from taking on board somebody's views in the heat of a real conversation.)

In a dialogue, people are **open with one another** — to an appropriate level, that is. The conversation takes place in a climate of mutual trust. In a dialogue, we feel that it is safe to talk about meaningful things — including our feelings — because we trust the other person not to take advantage. We are willing to share our views and talk about our confusion because we feel safe from attack or status games.

In a dialogue, people are **open to other people's views and ideas**. They are willing to be influenced by what they hear. This doesn't mean that you should not hold strong views, simply that you remain willing to consider what you hear. Without this openness, how can the communication be genuinely two-way? Keeping an open mind is the opposite to being dogmatic, prejudiced or narrow-minded.

Dialogues are **constructive**. They serve a **positive purpose**. They are productive and rewarding. They make life better in some way. The purpose of a conversation (or chunk of conversation) can be anything from 'having a pleasant time together' to 'explaining how to use a new piece of software' to 'sorting out a personal issue'. The process of a conversation is clearly related to its purpose. For example, a brainstorm conversation needs to follow a different process (or set of rules) from a decision-making conversation. If a conversation doesn't have a *positive* purpose, then it is likely to break down in some way. If the purpose of a conversation is wholly negative (e.g. to dole out unmitigated criticism), we should not be surprised if it fails to work.

Dialogues are **collaborative** rather than competitive interactions. In a dialogue, Person A and Person B cooperate to make the conversation serve its **positive purpose**. They build on one another's ideas rather than compete over them.

The participants in a dialogue treat each other as equals in terms of human worth. In other words, they communicate **on the level.** This does not mean that roles are irrelevant. The fact that one person is a teacher and the other is a pupil will inevitably influence the content of the conversation, but it should not prevent the teacher from treating the other person with the same consideration she wants for herself. (And the same for the pupil).

If person A considers himself or herself to be 'superior' to Person B in a fundamental way, the interaction can never be a dialogue. The fact is, we *all* react negatively (often strongly so) to behaviours we see as 'talking down' or devaluing, behaviours we consider to be condescending, judgemental, disdainful, supercilious, patronising, arrogant, demeaning, sarcastic, rude, dismissive or mocking.

People **manage their emotions** well in a dialogue. They might experience strong negative feelings but work hard at not letting these interfere with the process of communication. They find ways to express their anger without turning the conversation into a confrontation.

The case for placing Dialogue at the heart of our primary education system.

1. The ability to communicate effectively (to be good at dialogue) is the most fundamental of all life skills. This competency is too important to be just 'picked up' and should be taught explicitly and in depth from the earliest age.

Dialogue has been rightly called the 'key enabling tool of life'.

Just about every significant interaction we have — at home, at work, in our intimate relationships, with our friends, in the doctor's surgery, in emergencies, and so on — depends for its success (or failure) on verbal communication.

In the real world of living together and working together, spoken communication is overwhelmingly how we organise and experience our lives. It is how we build friendships, collaborate, negotiate, help and be helped, dig out information, create ideas . . . the list is endless.

I cannot think of any other set of cognitive/emotional/ behavioural skills that come close in importance to those required for effective interpersonal communication.

Yet as we stand today, it's possible to travel the entire educational journey, from primary school to university, without ever having specific lessons in interpersonal communication — the mother of all life skills.

A set of recommended teaching objectives for speaking and listening skills was introduced into the English primary school curriculum at the end of 2003 and these undoubtedly address some important areas of language development.

But the guidelines are inadequate when it comes to encouraging dialogue, as defined earlier. To grow into skilled and wise communicators, young people need to develop a practical understanding of human nature and the values that underpin successful interactions — like mutuality, immediacy, openness and self-discipline. They need to appreciate how people respond to each other, what role pride plays, how our feelings influence the way we listen, the importance of feeling valued, the need to check assumptions, the need to stay 'on task', and so on. Without these insights, it is impossible, I contend, for anyone to develop their communication competencies properly.

2. Growing up in a communication-rich environment is essential for a young person's social and emotional development. For many pupils, school is the best chance they have of experiencing these conditions.

For a large number of children, the classroom may provide them with the only opportunity they get to have positive communication experiences.

There is widespread evidence that more and more children are arriving at their primary schools with poorly developed communication competences, unfit to be taught. This is not a small-scale issue. A survey in the Times Education Supplement of 350 primary school Ofsted reports found that 50 per cent of them revealed unsatisfactory speaking and listening skills in 4 and 5 year olds. In a recent national survey, over 50 per cent of children said they would like to spend more time talking to their parents. In a poll by a leading speech therapy charity, 89 per cent of nursery workers said they were worried about the growth of speech, language and communication difficulties among preschool children. The story is the same wherever you look.

Research shows that children who enter nursery and school with inadequate language and communication skills are more likely to experience learning, behaviour and relationship problems compared to children who grow up in homes full of conversation.

It is not hard to allocate blame - too much time spent in front of the TV and games machine, the decline of talk within the busy modern family, the fragmented sound-bite culture of 21st century media, the shortage of positive role models in society, the substitution of texting and emailing for face-to-face conversation. The combination of these powerful influences has led to what David Bell, Chief Inspector of Schools, calls "a communication crisis among young people".

Inevitably, children experience very different quantities and qualities of conversation outside school and this clearly affects their attitudes and aptitudes. For example, studies have shown that in professional and middle class families, encouragement vastly outweighs discouragement as a conversational theme, while in many working class homes the ratio is reversed. It is no wonder that middle class children are six times more likely to aspire to go to university than their less economically-advantaged counterparts.

The language development of children can also vary enormously. Studies in America have shown that, by the age of 4, children of professional parents have up to twice as many words as working class children and up to four times as many as children from families on welfare.

One researcher has described how Britain is in danger of producing a "generation of zombies". Since it seems likely that the root causes of the problem are now a permanent feature of society, the need for schools to take responsibility for developing the dialogue skills of young people could not be greater.

3. Teaching with dialogue at its centre is the most effective form of teaching there can be. There needs to be a revolution in the classroom.

Dialogue is the most effective teaching tool there is. This is not wishful thinking but a highly researched conclusion. Dialogue (teacher/pupil and pupil/pupil) engages the brain. You cannot participate in a dialogue without thinking things through. It is not like answering a quiz or repeating facts. The benefits are many.

Better learning. Dialogic teaching stimulates children's thinking and advances their learning and understanding. This is because knowledge and understanding do not come from unquestioningly accepting somebody else's ideas but from thinking for yourself — weighing up the evidence, analysing the reasoning, exploring the alternatives. Thinking and language are inseparable. To be effective, teaching needs to provide pupils with a constant flow of interactions that engage them in cognitively-demanding conversations.

Better brains. The latest view of neuroscience is that talk is necessary for the physical as well as the intellectual development of the brain. The most important phase for the growth of the brain is the primary school years. This is when the brain develops its capacity for memory, learning and social-emotional intelligence. After this period, these processes come to a virtual standstill. Research shows that talk is by far the most effective way we have of fuelling this crucial developmental process.

Better assessment. A greater emphasis on dialogue in the classroom helps the teacher to get a much more accurate sense of how well an individual pupil is progressing. A proper conversation with a pupil will reveal far more information about a pupil's state of understanding than any number of quizzes.

Better engagement. The combination of well-planned oral work and collaborative activities are known to be much better at keeping children 'on task' than conventional written work. Teacher-dominated approaches (rote, recitation, exposition and so on) provide a strong sense of security because they enable teachers to stay in control of the ideas the lesson deals with. Unfortunately, they fail to engage the full attention and thinking capacity of pupils.

Better role modelling. The behaviours displayed by teachers using dialogic methods provide ideal role-model material for the pupils' own development, and so supplement the direct teaching of dialogue skills. Critical behaviours include listening attentively, taking other people's views seriously, responding constructively, probing for greater understanding, backing up views with reasoning and evidence, collaborating in problem solving and negotiation tasks, and so on.

What it's like in our primary schools today?

How well do our schools teach young people to use the power of communication to help them achieve their goals? How well do teachers use talk as part of their professional skill-set? After spending the past seven years researching the subject, I would say the answer is somewhere between 'not at all' and 'poorly'. There are exceptions, of course, but in my experience they are in a small minority.

In case you have not been to a primary school classroom lately, let me describe what I commonly see going on.

Long periods of time are spent in solitary reading, writing and drawing tasks. When there is talking, it is mostly done by the teacher. This does not mean, however, that pupils are listening. Some studies show that at any given moment only about 1 in 5 pupils are paying attention to what the teacher is saying. The others are lost in their own thoughts, looking out the window, and so on. Although the children are sometimes placed in groups, there is little going on by way of genuine collaborative working.

A lot of teacher talk follows ritualised forms. Recitation teaching is a good example, where the formula is: ask a question, get an answer, offer feedback. Teachers like to ask a lot of questions in order to 'engage' with as many pupils as possible. The quicker the response, the better the teacher likes it. This quiz-like approach gives the appearance of interactivity, although the questions are usually pretty undemanding, and often require only a single word answer. As a result, children get good at giving the right answers but not so good at thinking for themselves. If a child gives a wrong answer, the teacher tends to gloss over it because dealing with it might slow the 'pace' of the lesson, a obsession for many teachers who are under pressure to deliver 'lively' lessons.

Many children see the classroom as a place of risk. As a consequence, they develop good strategies for 'getting by' (or even being invisible) rather than openly engaging in the lesson. Many are reluctant to ask questions for fear of derision, ridicule or mockery — behaviours the teacher is often unaware of doing.

Teachers use a politically correct form of all-purpose praise to avoid any suggestion of criticism or discouragement. The praise is too bland and vague to have any relevance or impact.

Many of the children speak quietly, apologetically, or mumble their words. Some children speak hardly at all. When children *are* given a talking task, it's usually in the form of a one-way presentation, which is of very little benefit in helping to build the skills of dialogue.

What our classroom could be like

What might a classroom look like in an education system that emphasises dialogue?

I think the first thing we would notice is the way the children approach communication. Since they are used to being listened to, they talk clearly, confidently and enthusiastically. They are proud of their views and ideas. They make their points directly and explicitly rather than hinting at them or rambling. They bring their views to life with personal stories and examples. They happily speculate and make mistakes without shame or embarrassment.

The children listen well and routinely check their understanding. They are happy to admit if they do not understand something. The classroom is filled with energetic but disciplined discussion. Teachers and pupils have proper joined-up conversations rather than fragmented question-and-answer exchanges.

Large chunks of lessons in every subject are given over to dialogue. On many occasions, whole lessons are oral from start to finish. Oral work is seen as an end in itself, not just as a prelude to the real work of writing.

Teachers ask questions to encourage reasoning and speculation rather than a search for the right answers. Children are encouraged to take time to think before answering. Wrong answers aren't dismissed or glossed over but treated as useful stepping stones to better understanding.

Each child is treated as a valuable individual, with his or her own way of reaching understanding, and teachers provide them with honest, specific feedback on their intellectual, social and emotional development.

The children are ready for the revolution.

For the past five years, I have been a consultant to the BT Education Programme, which aims to help young people, their teachers and families develop a sound set of skills in spoken communication. The free resources provided by the programme (DVDs, online activities, workshops, lesson plans, teaching guides, classroom volunteers, funding schemes, etc.) are now being used in many thousands of schools (details at **www.bt.com/education**)

As part of the Programme, children throughout the UK have been devising their own classroom 'communication charters'. The list below is a compilation of the 12 most popular rules that have emerged from this exercise. It suggests to me that young people are more than ready for a future rich in dialogue.

1. We pay other people the same attention and consideration we expect for ourselves.
2. We share our views openly
3. We listen carefully to others
4. We talk one at a time and don't interrupt
5. We think before we speak
6. We back up our ideas with the reasoning behind them
7. We find out the facts rather than make assumptions
8. We check to make sure our understanding is correct
9. We keep an open mind
10. We ask questions if we don't understand
11. We make our conversations useful and enjoyable
12. We manage our emotions so they don't get in the way of communication

Andrew Bailey describes himself as a conversationologist, someone who 'studies the principles and practices of interpersonal communication'. He finds the way people interact an endlessly fascinating subject on which to write, lecture and run workshops. Andrew came to the field seven years ago after spending 25 years in the mass media businesses, first as a journalist and later as an advertising creative director and television producer/writer. He is the co-author with Professor Gerard Egan of two books on the skills and wisdom of dialogue. Andrew is the co-founder of Dialogics, which produces educational resources on behalf of the BT Education Programme to help young people, parents and teachers develop their communication competencies.

References.

How Children Fail by John Holt, *Penguin*
The Skilled Helper by Gerard Egan, *Brooks/Cole*
Words and Rules by Steven Pinker, *Science Masters*
Culture and Pedagogy by Robin Alexander, *Blackwell*
Emotional Literacy Handbook by Antidote, *David Fulton Publishers*
Words and Minds by Neil Mercer, *Routledge.*

STRANGER THAN FICTION?

Barry Fryer

If a week is a long time in politics, 50 years is an aeon in education. 10 years ago, hardly anyone had a digital camera or mobile phone. 20 years ago, I typed my first book on a BBC micro with its miniscule 32k memory. The publishers asked for a hard copy; they couldn't do electronic typesetting. 30 years ago, the PC did not exist and no one had even anticipated the internet.

It's easier to create fiction than make a reliable prediction. But, all too often, both fiction and prediction are useless in forecasting the future. So, whilst it's intriguing to speculate about education in 2055, it will probably be different from anything we can possibly imagine. With this proviso, here is one scenario.

Education in 2055

Pupils and students no longer go to school or college. They can learn in bed or while going for a jog. Most things they need to know or want to know are available through a vastly improved internet and can be accessed using biotronics. Since 2045, this multidisciplinary technology has used tiny learning cards pushed into an implant behind the pupil's ear. However, these are giving way to implants that have their own built-in molecular PCs with wireless megaband connections to the net. The implants link the internet to the memory regions of the brain, making a vast array of learning programmes and databases available to students.

Information can be accessed anywhere, any time, at the press of a fingertip behind the ear! Pupils see the material, in their mind's eye, as it were. The entire curriculum and associated learning materials are available to them. Pupils remember much of the material, with the help of memory-enhancing drugs. But anything they do forget is available in an instant from the net or from the implant's own huge

61

memory.

Learning technical and social skills and attitudes uses the same biotronic channel, but draws on advanced inherent reality software to model a wide range of skill and attitude-shaping interactions, using virtual actors in computer-generated simulations.

The new implant can also scan the brain, allowing rapid electronic assessment of pupils' learning and general intellectual development.

Researchers are currently working on improvements to the more problematic suites of programs, those dealing with attitude shaping, behaviour change and student assessment. Employers are getting to grips with computer-generated student attainment profiling, which is rapidly replacing conventional selection tests and examinations.

This may sound like science fiction, but biotronics already exists, as biology and electronics come together at the micro and molecular levels. But even if education in 50 years time is nothing like this, we can be certain that it will be profoundly different from its present form. Humanity has reached a critical point, a period that will lead to breakthrough or breakdown. In education, the media-related technologies are certain to make what happens in the classroom look outdated and mundane. Students will increasingly find classroom learning tedious and pedestrian, compared with what is available through the media.

One reason students may not go to school or college in 50 years time is that educating them at home will be much cheaper. Media and IT professionals, such as TV programme producers and software and web program writers, will use technology to replace teachers altogether and offer stunning, low-cost interactive packages of knowledge and skills learning. Computer-generated 'actors' may replace teachers in building students' cognition, social skills and behaviour. Contact with peers may increasingly be by electronic means too, with far less personal interaction.

Assessment will probably change radically, both in terms of

what is assessed and how. A brain scan might replace written examinations. Exams themselves may become outdated. Biotronic measurements of development, perhaps in terms of brain cell growth and differentiation, may become the yardsticks for future employment, replacing traditional exam-based certification.

The future governance of education is especially difficult to foretell. We are accustomed to oscillating policies, which swing between tighter control and more relaxed monitoring. These swings will probably persist, with unending policy changes, strategy reversals and continual renaming and re-organising of institutions and education management structures.

Challenging assumptions

Whatever the future, it will challenge some of our core assumptions. Many of them may not survive. We can deal with the first three together:

Assumption 1: *Teachers will carry on teaching*
Assumption 2: *Teaching will take place in the classroom*
Assumption 3: *Students will attend a place called 'school' or 'college'*

There has to be a serious question mark about whether the teacher or the classroom will survive the probable developments in human learning systems, given the technologies which are already developing fast.

We can expect a development like biotronics to be well established by 2055. There will be some way of creating an interface between the learner's brain and vast electronic databases and virtual reality experiences. Much learning will therefore use this technology. Teaching will be replaced by learning management, where advisors and mentors help students to set targets, plan their learning experiences and prepare for assessments. This has already started to happen, especially in Higher Education.

There will be problems. Motivating some pupils might be a key issue. New strategies may be needed to ensure that pupils pursue learning and don't stay in bed or play computer games all day. Then there is the problem that if most education happens at home, who will supervise it? Perhaps, by 2055, parents and guardians will mostly work from home; or homes may have their own robotic tutor.

Future learning will probably start sooner and progress faster than it does now. We might expect to see primer level learning for under-3s, giving them a flying start; basic modules for 3-5 year olds; intermediate learning for 5-9 year olds; whilst advanced learners are the 9-12 year olds. *Research methods* and *World of work* learning sets are available for 12+ year olds. By 2055, most pupils will probably be physically and emotionally mature by the age of 12, and will be seeking employment or postgraduate research posts in their early teens. But postgrad jobs may be rare, as there may be little left to discover!

Whatever happens, the future will change the teacher's role drastically and leave little place for the traditional classroom. Students will need to be taught how to use the internet effectively and sort out reliable material from junk. But what will probably be needed most of all are learning activities which compensate for the social impairment of children growing up without adequate interaction with their peers and role models.

We needn't speculate about whether this will be true. It already is. Children are spending more time in front of TVs and PCs; and less in contact with their families and peers. Poor social skills among children are already a problem. Family conversation is disappearing. Parents and children are finding it hard to share personal concerns and problems. If the trend continues, a major challenge for education in 2055 will be to find ways to teach children how to live and work together, create caring relationships and perform well in teams.

Assumption 4: The knowledge explosion will continue
Assumption 5: We should teach skills rather than facts

These assumptions are linked. The information explosion, in which new knowledge constantly raises doubts about old knowledge, has been used to justify the argument that knowledge is obsolescent. The conclusion often drawn is that we should focus on teaching skills rather than facts, because facts become outdated, but skills don't.

There are at least three problems with this assumption. Firstly, the knowledge explosion may soon be over. There is no reason to assume that the exponential growth of information will continue indefinitely. Within a few decades, we may have discovered almost everything there is to know and rebutted most of the misinformation we live with now. Then we will no longer be able to claim that knowledge is obsolescent.

Secondly, we must guard against the temptation to treat knowledge as less important than skills. Knowledge is becoming more reliable as myths, errors and confusions are dispelled. And deep, accurate knowledge is a vital ingredient of 'expertise', an attribute enjoyed by outstanding achievers and highly creative people. New insights and innovations rarely arise from ignorance. People who achieve exceptional creativity and success usually have very good knowledge of their fields or they are good at seeing connections with knowledge from other fields.

Thirdly, we must be careful about assuming that skills are somehow generic - universal and unalterable. As knowledge changes, skills change too. Emerging disciplines require new skills, and existing skills need to be revised as our understanding of the world improves.

In 50 years, there will probably be something with a name like the knowledge set. It will consist of facts that have been verified and are reasonably immutable. Gone will be the days of abundant conjectures, hypotheses and theories, endlessly disputed. Society will have thrown out the weaker ideas and those that remain will be stable. The rate at which new knowledge appears may slow to a trickle. Step change may be a thing of the past. Groundbreaking inventions might become a rarity. Innovations could mostly be small refinements to existing artefacts and systems. By the mid 21st century, there may be no new domains to discover and no major battles over ideas.

If these things happen, a major role for educators will be to build students' citizenship skills; to enable them to lead fulfilling lives; to train them to contest prejudice and discrimination; and learn to manage relationships as well as technologies.

Assumption 6: The world will continue to develop along broadly similar lines

This assumption is dangerous and almost certainly false. World politics may shift dramatically. We may seriously deplete the environment. Thousands of species will probably become extinct. Storms may rage and new deserts open up. Terrorism might become endemic. Anti-social behaviour may be pervasive. Inequalities may be acute.

Fiction? Not if we fail to tackle today's most pressing problems. Many people are complacent about social, political, economic and environmental problems, but the next generation of pupils and students will have to get to grips with what went wrong with the world and what must be done to prevent total breakdown. So, while pupils learn Physics and Maths alongside *The collapse of progress* and *The sociology of the family meal table*, they may be wondering how their parents and grandparents let the world get into the state it's in.

Assumption 7: The aims of education are largely understood and are being achieved

The 20th century saw an explosion of interest in, and

debate about, educational objectives. But did it produce the right answers? Among the ideas thrashed out were education as a preparation: 1] for life, 2] for the world of work, and 3] for citizenship.

The writings of Carl Rogers and others encouraged tutors to think about the importance of having unconditional positive regard for students and of helping them maximise their personal growth, by pursuing autonomy and 'self-actualisation'. Many teachers implicitly assumed that, given the freedom to learn, students would do good things and pursue worthy goals. Comparatively little was said about what to do if students choose to turn their backs on established morals and pursue purely selfish goals or anti-social conduct.

In parallel, there developed an assumption that education was primarily about preparing young people for jobs, rather than for life as a whole. This has led to a situation in which many students can now operate a powerful PC, but can't boil an egg; they know the dangers of saturated fat, but fill themselves with junk food; they know the structure of DNA, but can't make a distinction between the verbs *effect* and *affect*.

The way ahead?

We can be certain that education will be drastically different in 2055. It could be even more like fiction than these predictions suggest. The changes will probably create as many problems as they solve.

It seems quite likely that there will be no schools, colleges or classrooms. Teaching as we know it may disappear, replaced by less expensive mediated learning, broadcast on some super-web. Knowledge may have stabilised, with few breakthroughs and hardly any new domains to study. Students will probably have managers and mentors rather than tutors, guiding them through a vast array of online resources, supplemented by periodic group activities at a wide variety of venues.

What should happen to education, if we are to manage such changes?

1   Education must fully embrace the knowledge economy and take control of its technologies, harnessing the potential to improve learning, within a less structured framework. It should routinely use technology and mediated learning to enable students to acquire knowledge and some skills.

2   When students do get together 'face-to-face' with mentors and peers, learning should focus more on attitudes, social skills and group problem solving abilities. There is much room for improvement in these areas.

3   Education must find better ways of developing students' advanced thinking skills, starting at an early age. Learning to think is currently given much less attention than it deserves.

4   We will need to find imaginative ways to motivate students to learn more independently of the classroom and take greater responsibility for their careers and life choices. Mentoring may be central to this.

5   More attention must be given to developing life skills and citizenship skills, such as the ability to form close relationships, cook a dinner or care for a child. Currently, these sorts of learning are neglected. As a result, students find it easy to learn physics, history or electronics, but hard to relate to their families and other people.

6   Education should take a stronger moral stand, imposing more robust social and ethical boundaries on personal freedom, helping students to differentiate goodwill from ill-will and value the needs of others above self-gratification.

In future, we will have an even greater need for exceptional, imaginative education that enables people to solve intransigent problems, cement together their societies and groups, and forge greater empathy, respect, trust and cooperation. We will need an education system which creates a more integrated and tolerant society and combats the drift towards division, alienation and uncertainty, not to mention disintegration of the physical environment.

Barry Fryer, MA, MSc, MCMI, FRSA is a freelance writer, consultant and senior associate of The Creativity Centre Ltd. He specialises in designing innovative learning materials. He was formerly a professor and assistant dean of faculty at Leeds Metropolitan University, where he worked for more than 20 years. Barry is author of *The Practice of Construction Management*, a book now in its 4th edition, which addresses the human side of construction management. He has written other book chapters and some 30 articles, mainly in professional journals and magazines, and mostly dealing with human relations, innovative management and management education.

AN ENTERPRISING EDUCATION

Gerard Darby

You might remember hearing about a pedestrian bridge in London that was opened to coincide with the new Millennium. People came in droves to admire its elegant design and walk across it. However, a problem arose in that they were able to hear the footsteps of the other people walking across and as a result would unconsciously fall into the same pace, a bit like soldiers falling into a march. The result was that this exerted pressure on the bridge so that it began to sway to the rhythm of those walking. The more that people walked the same way, the more it swayed. As a consequence, it had to be closed whilst the architects and engineers argued as to whose fault it was.

I have always been fascinated by those people who don't follow the crowd and instead walk in a different direction, to a different rhythm and with a different pace. Unfortunately, they are often dismissed as eccentrics, weirdos, cranks and worse. A few years ago, I interviewed forty-four inventors and entrepreneurs to try and uncover their common traits and ways of thinking. Whilst they had very diverse approaches and ideas, the one thing they all seemed to have in common was that they or their ideas were initially dismissed as being crazy.

Breaking free from the ranks isn't what society is geared towards. It seems much more concerned with the maintenance of the status quo and with conformity and uniformity. Whilst enterprise, creativity and innovation are buzzwords liberally bandied about by government, industry and public bodies, there is a huge chasm between the rhetoric and the reality.

This is blatantly demonstrated by today's education system which is focussed on teaching young people to come up with the right answer. It has been estimated that by the time the average person finishes college, he or she will have taken over

2,600 tests, quizzes and exams (1) - most often to find the so-called right answer. But what is the right answer? Generally it tends to be whatever happens to be in the teacher's head at the time or written in the answerbook.

In life, as opposed to the classroom, we generally have to find or create our own answers and what may be the right answer in one particular time or situation, often isn't in another. In reinventing education, I believe we should encourage a child to find an answer because in doing so he/she has to explore, question, experiment, analyse, investigate, interpret and evaluate information and these are invaluable competencies for the demands of our modern world. At the same time, to do these things effectively the child has to be engaged and that is something our current education system is failing to do. Young people today are voting with their feet about their schooling and it is estimated that 400,000 are playing truant on any one day (2)

Education's fixation with the right answer makes me recall a story about a student's response to a question in a physics examination that asked: "Show how it is possible to determine the height of a tall building with the aid of a barometer." The answer in the physics teacher's head was to measure the air pressure at the bottom and top of the building and then apply the appropriate formula, which illustrates that pressure reduces as height increases. However, a student on his examination paper put, "Take the barometer to the top of the building, attach a long rope to it, and lower the barometer to the ground. Then, bring it back up, measuring the length of the rope and barometer and this will give the height of the building."

The physics teacher couldn't discount this answer but felt that the student needed to demonstrate an understanding of physics and so was given another opportunity with the problem. This time the student put, "Take the barometer to the top of the building. Lean over the edge of the roof, drop the barometer, timing its fall with a stopwatch. Then, using the formula $S=1/2at$, calculate the height of the building."

The student went on to offer several other potential solutions including taking the barometer out on a sunny day and then by measuring the height of the barometer, the length of its shadow and the building's shadow use simple proportion to measure the height of the building. The answer I liked best, as it appeals to my enthusiasm for lateral thinking, was to take the barometer to the basement, knock on the superintendent's door and when he answers say, "Mr Superintendent, I have here a fine barometer. If you tell me the height of this building, I will give you this barometer."

The importance of failure

So what about the wrong answer or seemingly wrong answer? I would argue that failing is not the terrible thing that education and society makes it out to be, particularly in the way that it stigmatises those that fail. Failure within our present education system certainly does not equate to failure later in life. In my opinion, education has become so preoccupied with success that it has missed the fundamental point about failure - that is an unavoidable, almost necessary, part of success. In researching this article, I asked a number of entrepreneurs about their views on education. Inventor and entrepreneur James Dyson asserted that you need to fail in order to learn how to succeed:

"Although I had the initial idea in the beginning of the cyclone with the vacuum cleaner, in order to make it work I had to go through 5,124 failures. Those failures sound awful and depressing but actually they're the reverse. Each one is exciting and you learn such a huge amount from failure. I've got this theory that in a number of subjects at school – obviously in design and technology – you should give people more marks according to the number of failures they make because you learn from failures, you don't learn from success."

In tandem with education's emphasis on success and being right, there is too much of a focus on knowledge of information (know-that) and not enough on skills and competencies (know-how). For today's world, a young person needs to learn not only to find answers, but also how to develop questions.

In reinventing education, we also need to impress upon young people that they can't know everything and instead help them develop a self-awareness to recognise the gaps in their knowledge, understanding and skills. The entrepreneurs that I have come across often cite this ability, as they put it 'to know what you don't know' as a crucial competency that young people should develop. With the internet and other technologies, the challenge today isn't any longer about acquiring knowledge and information; it is much more about being able to determine which information is accurate, how the information can be used and when it would be most effective to act on it.

Sadly, despite young people being exposed to much more information, they do not seem to be creating more opportunities as a result of it. In part, I believe this is because as a society we no longer value the time to reflect and process all the information that we receive and in part because we fail to inculcate a mindset that encourages risk-taking and endeavour.

Learning to learn

As well as enabling students to develop awareness to know what they don't know, education should enthuse them to discover the things they didn't know they needed to know – something that should be at the very heart of learning. We are not teaching young people how to learn or conveying the excitement of learning. Sean Blair, an entrepreneur and trustee of the RSA which started the Campaign for Learning, puts it very eloquently:

"One of the critical failures of the current education system is we don't learn how to learn. We don't learn what learning is. I was hugely inspired by Charles Handy who said 'those that are in love with learning are in love with life' and in my early twenties I actually understood what learning is. I think a huge shift would be when children actually stopped to reflect and learn about learning. Then learning is something very different. It isn't something that grown ups throw at you – something you've got to do. Instead it becomes a key to curiosity and vitality and with it you can do anything."

Coupled with a need to develop an understanding of the process of learning, we need to inculcate an ability to think. As James Dyson notes, "Very few marks are given for original thinking, for seriously thinking ideas out for yourself and expressing them. That is why I think design and technology is important for everyone because it teaches you the creative process."

Whilst such original thinking and creativity may not be valued within education, the only option to an individual to devise a product that is significantly different to others on the market is their creative approach to it. A company that wants to survive in our uncertain times will need to be constantly inventive and adaptable.

Whenever creativity in education is discussed, the focus tends to be on how to unleash the creative talents of the children. I would also like to see the focus extend to include how the innate creativity of teachers can be allowed to flourish. Teachers, in my opinion, often get the raw deal with the accusing finger pointing at them as if they are the ones holding the children back, rather than the bureaucratic constraints that they have to work with. Teachers are highly creative. They need to be in order to break down complex issues so that young people can understand them, to adjust to the differing levels of students, to make lessons intriguing and to develop engaging materials.

In reinventing education, we have to develop a culture that is conducive for creativity otherwise we will fail to attract creative individuals into the classroom. We are suffering a severe shortage of design and engineering teachers and thereby our children are suffering a shortfall in their creative ability as a result.

Special needs are special

In liberating the creativity of teachers, we might also see a shift towards a learning culture that not only accepts but celebrates different learning styles. For example, whilst a lot has progressed within education with support available to students with special learning difficulties such as dyslexia, I would argue that too much of the support is orientated towards trying to get the dyslexic young person to think in a manner that will fit in with our existing way of teaching and learning, rather than trying to work with their unique learning style. There isn't recognition that dyslexia can actually be a benefit and that it essentially entails a different way of thinking - one that if fostered can be extraordinarily productive.

A surprising high number of entrepreneurs are dyslexic and I believe this is no coincidence. As well as having to develop a tenacity and resilience in their attitudes - traits extremely valuable in enterprise - I believe dyslexia enables them to make leaps in their thinking and thereby innovate. Recently, I talked to an entrepreneur who was dyslexic and he told me that he hoped that there wouldn't be a cure for dyslexia because he attributed his ability to develop new and exciting ideas to it.

We still do not appreciate or value diversity in its truest sense. Yes, we have started to come to recognise the value of ethnic and social diversity, but not diversity in terms of different ways of thinking, different ideas and different behaviours. Such diversity confounds and questions the system that education revolves around and that is perhaps my biggest bugbear about education – that it is a system. In every respect it is designed as a system – administratively, culturally and even physically. But systems rely on everyone thinking and behaving the same way; the world would not be such an enthralling and inspiring place if they did.

Demis Hassabis, who did his GCSEs at 14, his A Levels at 16 and at 21 founded a computer games company, believes that the education system is unable to cope with people like him: "It seems to me a lot of resource is being put into catering for people who are not doing so well, for whatever reasons. I think it's good the work that is being done there. But I think hardly any resource is being put comparatively into a kid who is way ahead of his class or is not being stimulated for positive reasons such as they're too good or they're too fast. What do we do for those kids? It seems that they're left to fend for themselves at the moment. A little bit like I was. A lot of them if they're determined enough will find their own way. But they might get disillusioned and never make it. I know a lot of people, very talented people, but they have never been exposed to enough things so they have never found a passion and that means they can never fully express their talents".

As well as failing to value diversity, we don't seem to value or even want to try and value less measurable and definable skills such as interpersonal communication skills and people skills. I admit that the latter is a rather nebulous umbrella term that encompasses a whole range of abilities (but crucial ones) including the capacity to work with, manage, motivate and develop other people. Whilst these may not be skills valued in education, they are craved for by companies.

Charlie Osbourne, entrepreneur and co-founder of the consultancy Fresh Minds, an agency that he and a friend started in their early twenties to provide businesses with the untapped potential of undergraduates and recent graduates, believes people skills are crucial: "Life and the world is about people. Everything you do is about people and understanding people is the most important skill in life. Developing people skills is so important."

There are many other such competencies that education needs to foster. Caroline Plumb, the other founder of Fresh Minds, told me that education not only needs to develop an ability for pupils to see both sides of an argument, but also for them to then be able to take a stance on an issue and defend it, "The British education system is very concerned with the debate around an argument, but only the debate and never taking a position and that's not very helpful in business because at some point you've got to make the call."

Breaking down the boundaries

If we are to reinvent education for today's complex and exciting world then many of the boundaries in it will need to be removed – the boundary between the school and the community, the boundary between formal and informal learning, the boundaries between subject areas such as science and art (think what extraordinary ideas could be unleashed if you bring these two disciplines together), the boundary between physical and mental agility (why do we not place the same emphasis on exercising and training the mind as we do the body?) and the artificial boundaries between the teacher and the student.

The role of the teacher is changing. Technology has made that almost inevitable with students now being able to use the internet and other communication tools to find out and learn about things. Indeed, children are often able to make use of the available technologies more proficiently and adeptly than their teachers. The very premise of education is being turned on its head with the student now being able to lead their own learning. Perhaps we are going back to what education should be all about. Education literally means to lead from within and maybe that is where a reinvention of education needs to start – from within the student and their motivations, their needs and their view of the world.

Tom Hadfield, who started his first business Soccernet at home when he was thirteen, told me that he got much more learning and inspiration outside of formal education, "I was getting much more of a life experience outside school. And should that be the case? Should you have to go off and find your life experience when you are a teenager growing up or should school somehow integrate you with all that is going on out there? I found school very constrained in what we were allowed to develop interest in."

Enterprise skills are life skills

It could be argued to what extent should you alter education to accommodate the needs of a small minority, albeit a growing one, of individuals who will go on to become inventors or entrepreneurs. However enterprise skills are life skills. The characteristics needed by the entrepreneur in terms of self-belief, creativity, ability to manage and adapt to change, seize opportunities and to communicate effectively are surely skills needed by most individuals whether working for themselves, for other people or in public service.

At the same time patterns of working life are changing drastically. Today's young people need to be more flexible, resourceful and resilient in their attitudes and outlook to thrive in a business environment where change and uncertainty are the norm. We're also going to be relying much more on their inventive talents. The population of the UK is ageing. The 2001 census showed that for the first time there are more people over the age of 60 than under the age of 16. It is a trend that is projected to continue, and by 2051 it is estimated that one in four people will be over the age of 65.

Moreover the legacy that we are leaving young people to inherit – global warming and other potential environmental catastrophes, a pension fund that may not have sufficient funds to support an increasing older population, a health service that will have to be continuously more efficient to cope with the growing demands on it - all of these problems will require enterprising and creative solutions from our younger generations.

But can enterprise be taught? Isn't it essentially an instinct? I am inclined to side with Oscar Wilde, who claimed, "Things worth knowing, can't be taught". I am not sure that some of the fundamental competencies needed for today's world such as lateral thinking, adaptability, vision, foresight and resourcefulness, can actually be taught - but they can certainly be learnt. They largely require an environment that is conducive for discovery, experimentation and risk-taking and thereby enables such behaviours to flourish.

I have found that a high number of entrepreneurs come

from families where a parent was also an entrepreneur. However, I don't believe this is due to a genetic predisposition to enterprise but rather that their family environment tolerated, if not excelled in, the highs and lows, triumphs and disasters, uncertainties and excitements resulting from their entrepreneurial pursuits.

In reinventing education, I believe that an important focus needs to be on the development of the environment and culture for effective learning. I am mindful that two very successful learning projects supported by NESTA (the National Endowment for Science, Technology and the Arts) are concerned with developing an effective environment for learning. In Bolton, the UK's first Technical Innovation Centre provides a literally 'hands-on' environment for children to learn about science and technology by allowing them to interact and experiment with exciting new technologies.

Up in Fort William, in a quite deprived area in the Highlands of Scotland, a different learning environment has been developed at Caol Primary School. There an independent art studio, Room 13, has been developed which is run like any normal business but the difference is that it is managed entirely by the young people (aged eight to 11 years) from the school. The children are responsible for everything from electing the officials to even paying the salaries of the two artists-in-residence. They also have the freedom to leave their classwork at any point, providing their coursework is up to date, and to go to Room 13 and exercise their imaginations. It is an approach that has had a very positive impact on their creativity with some of the children from the school having gone on to win the Barbie Art Prize - the children's version of the Turner Prize.

It may seem rather fluffy and trivial to place such an emphasis on the learning environment and culture, but consider some of the ironies of our existing school environments: we want children to develop their imaginations and creativity but their school surroundings are dull. We want pupils to learn to eat healthily but the food served up to them at school is unwholesome. We want young people to be excited about science, engineering and technology but the equipment we give them to learn such disciplines is often out of date.

The most important people in education

I don't pretend to have the right answer for reinventing education; rather, you need to search for answers - in the plural. Just as an inventor and entrepreneur experiments, takes risks and pushes boundaries, so you need to do the same with education, to make their learning relevant, inspiring and meaningful, without putting the young person's education at risk. Currently, we are risking young people's education on outdated and irrelevant forms of learning that ignore the needs of the fast-changing world that they are growing up in.

Successful businesses are ones that put the consumer at the heart of their operation. Similarly successful learning should put the student at the core. In reinventing education, let us focus on the most important people in education – the students. Let us value them as they truly are, as individuals with individual ideas, thoughts and aspirations and who, given the right encouragement and environment, could deliver an enterprising future for us all.

Gerard Darby is a researcher, writer and trainer specialising in enterprise, creativity and lateral thinking.

He was the first RSA Onians Fellow for which he undertook research on the motivations, characteristics and challenges of young entrepreneurs in the UK. In 2004, in follow-up research, he examined the challenges that a young person faces in sustaining and growing an enterprise in the UK and this was published by the RSA and the enterprise education charity businessdynamics (www.rsa.org.uk/acrobat/youngentrepreneurs.pdf)

Gerard has written two guides for young people who wish to develop an idea into a business: *The Little Book for Big Ideas* published in 2003 and the NESTA publication *Dare to Dream* published in 2004.

References

(1) Roger von Oech "A Whack on the Side of the Head" (1998, Warner Bros., New York)
(2) Audit Commission, 1999

EMBODIED CHOICES & VOICES

Penelope A. Best

'Life, like science and art, is a theory about the world: a theory that in our case takes bodily form... if those theories are good enough, then life will prosper and multiply; but if they are outmoded by changing conditions, their embodiments will dwindle and perish' Prelude (1)

I believe passionately in locating the body centrally within learning experiences. In this I mean the body-in-relation, in relation to itself, to the environment and to others, the social world, in effect socio-physical events. My personal and professional experiences support this view as I am situated within the world of dance, arts therapy, and creative process research. Each of these areas focuses upon processes between people and their worlds, their internal and external worlds. In turn these worlds are peopled.

When I give presentations and workshops for counselors, therapists, teachers, lecturers and artist practitioners I always offer opportunities to connect with simple bodily awareness. For me the starting point for reflection and sharing of information stems from oneself, one's here-and-now bodily response and room for maneuver. This bodily response is made up of personal history, present context, social expectations including issues of difference such as power, gender, ethnicity and ability. Bodily response and experience is complex and at the same time simple, in that it is simply in, and of, that moment, while 'meaning making' continues well beyond. What we do with this as educators, learners, artists, therapists, is crucial. What opportunities we give ourselves and others to explore relationship, beginning with an acknowledgement of how we mutually influence the bodily experience of the other. How do we literally shape each other through physical, social and contextual interaction (2)?

We learn-in-relation. And yet both traditional and contemporary education systems seem to go out of their way to fragment experience and uncouple body-mind connections. While early years education values full body learning, recent increased testing in primary schools and above has once again shifted the focus from learning to knowing, from experiencing to showing.   My concern is far wider than early years education as I feel opportunities for embodied learning are being missed at all stages; the body is quite literally being squeezed out. Technological developments have increased distance learning which is designed to widen participation.   However, this may also have a knock on effect of distancing our relationships to our bodily experiences unless we build in reference to, experience of, and reflection upon somatic information.

How can we harness new methods of communicating, sharing information, and learning which engage the whole person? How can we ensure that we literally embed the body within learning experiences, encourage access to the deep resources which are held within?   Adding physical sessions (PE, dance, sport) while important, is not the answer. Integration of the physical with the intellectual throughout education at all stages is vital for the future and by all stages, I mean secondary, tertiary and lifelong learning, as well as primary. In effect it would be re-integration, as there would need to be substantial change to classrooms, learning environments, criteria of learning, assessments and values.   Without this I envisage a de-socializing metamorphosis in which individuals are separated from one another while carrying massive thumbs and huge eyes and little else! There will be less appreciation of difference and the valuing of others.

In the future we need to monitor both individual body experience as a resource, where a learner might be alone at home on a computer, yet in a web chat room, as well as monitor the shared interactive body experience, where the learner is in the presence of others in a classroom.   While the kinesthetic may be viewed as only one of the multiple intelligences, a mode of knowing or entry point to learning (3), we must remember that we all have bodies. However, we may not all be musicians, artists or mathematicians.   Educators may be aware that every experience is filtered through bodily senses (4), yet few of us may realize that these senses are limited and shaped by evolution and focused upon survival pattern recognition (5). We are already developing current innovations such as robotic intelligences, virtual worlds, more distance learning, and implanted microchip communication all of which emerge from present body parameters. How can we create new embodied choices, in which individual learners have opportunities to experience and reflect on different perspectives and resources shaped by shifting positions, both physically and intellectually? (6) Can we provide sufficient space, time and materials for active shifts which would offer enriched possibilities for embodied reflections on learner's current choices and on new opportunities for growth and change?

These are difficult questions to answer and many are rhetorical at this point. However, I feel it appropriate within the context of this book for me to consider some of the ways in which my concerns might be met in the future. I consider two interlinked points, one is assessment and the other is the learner's physical involvement. As education, learning centres and opportunities widen through technology, I assume that there will still be a need for assessing the efficacy of what is on offer, no matter how dispersed. This assessment serves to satisfy the provider, the funder, and also the learner.

I have always found the learning process difficult to assess, since my days as a choreography lecturer when we had to find ways of pinning down creativity. I have learned over time to be extremely careful about criteria within assessment, to take time to create criteria which is sufficiently focused, yet also allows varied ways of evidencing learning. Over the past 12 years with colleagues within a dance movement therapy training programme (7), I have co-created numerous wonderful assignments and learning experiences for students which involved them in producing unique records of their learning processes using learning profiles, reflective essays, co-presentations and also drawings, sand trays and collages. However, we found that the more useful and pertinent an assignment became in supporting the student's learning, the harder it was for us to assess it! The individual nature of each production meant it took an inordinate amount of tutor time to adequately respect the student's reflective work. One very successful method was the introduction of triangulated peer, self and tutor assessments which included interaction and reflective discussion after observing a live event, literally a live performance of learning, with the body of the learner on show, in the moment. The live learner's body was central and essential to the task and this might inform ideas for integrating embodiment and assessment of learning.

I suggest that in the future it will be even more imperative to keep the learner's body as central to both learning and assessment. Assessment enables learning to be tangible, to be articulated, and it is important that this articulation is not solely verbal or text. As future educators (or learning supporters) we need to demonstrate that we value the embodiment of learning by accepting physical evidence of learning as valid. We can make use of webcams and mobile technology to co-create learning assignments. Students could be required to experience tasks before reporting back and discussing them from their own unique perspective as well as that of with others. We might develop the use of self-assessment with videos as evidence of bodily engagement. Each assignment could require investigation with tangible objects as well as websites, encouraging connections between the virtual and real worlds. In text, students could be encouraged to use more metaphoric and storied language within their work based upon their unique bodily perceptions. Valuing this sensory-perceptual relationship is as relevant to maths and sciences as to the humanities. Playing with ideas needs to be predicated upon playing with things, holding three dimensional objects which inform us about our own three dimensionality, our ups and our downs, our ins and our outs, our backwards and our forwards. The future may be viewed as a time element, yet it is also a space element and it is with us already (8) .

It is telling that within this short piece I have already felt so constrained by the dominant academic paradigm of written communication. I sense that I could have presented my ideas so much more richly and effectively in person, bodily with the non verbal support of movement, audience reaction, inflection and interaction. I would also have used a metaphoric landscape filled with my own somatically shaped symbols (9). However, as the context for this piece is a book, I decided to play with creating a short poem about my concerns. I chose the medium as it offered an opportunity to shape my words, open spaces and add questions as I would if I were speaking with you face to face. I have not written a poem since I was a child when the expectations were simple descriptive rhymes. My bodily response when I initially considered writing a poem was one of shrinking from possible judgment, feeling the discerning reader may find flaws. This narrowing of kinesphere, shrinking of posture, quite literally making myself smaller, can be a common response of learners (or the complete opposite one of enlarging one's chest like a blowfish, ready to attack). (10) These features hold information for both the individual and the system about what might be needed to create a 'good enough' holding environment. (11) I overcame my physical narrowing and restriction of breath by consciously breathing in, shifting my shape and deciding to ask the reader not to look for technical or aesthetic merit, but rather to share one way in which I can give my thoughts body.

'We cannot come to apprehend external reality except through the instrument of the body. Yet we cannot come to make sense of this apprehended reality except through the processes of the mind.' (12)

Embodied choices

So, there are institutional bodies, bodies of knowledge
Governmental bodies, professional bodies, busy bodies
But where are the a-live presences, the lived-in bodies
*   Of the learners? As experts? As teachers?*

We live through our bodies

We learn through our bodies
In space, in time, in relation to gravity, in relation to others (13)...
These are givens, aren't they?
　　And yet they seem to be taken away... by education

Squeezing out the bodies, to fit in the computers
Fragmented splitting of mind from body, body from mind,
"Eyes on the screen, fingers on the button
Butts on seats, hands in the air!"
　　Lip service to experiential learning (14)

Where is the body central to the process of inquiry? (15)
The body constituting a mode of knowing
Personal epistemology born out of touching the world
The body in touch... out of touch ... touching ... others
　　My world? your world? our world? whose world?
　　A virtual world?

Can we really still be limping with a Cartesian fracture?
In our brave, less –than- new world of chaos, complexity, and unity in diversity?
In which 'widening participation' may in fact mean less deepening
Where more and more people are less and less connected
　　To themselves, to others
To cultural embodiment, subtle somatic knowing
　　Of rich, rich differences

While the movement impulse may be the root of thought, of language (16)
Movement alone is not enough ... relationship is essential
　'Against' relationships as well as 'with' relationships
　　Expression, deconstruction, reconstruction, social construction
　　Deep structures, meaning making

(my! what a lot of physical building!)
In relation to others

To experience 'Otherness', to push up against, to define, to
reach an edge
A defining edge, a perceived discrepancy
Which provides just the right amount of sensed difference
    to make a difference (17)
        to generate a precious moment of learning

Body play, playing with ideas, playing with risk, playing with
the unknown
Creatively inquiring, testing, challenging, checking,
    With whatever body we have, whatever abilities
        Somatic inquiry... encouraging choices...using our
body voices

Breath in... breath out... reflect, connect...connect and reflect...
fully
Valuing inspiration ... voicing choice...quite literally
    And fully... full bodied engagement
        We are in, and of, our bodies whatever age we are
        Let's shout it out!

' **Keeping alive the movement impulse - the root of
all development of a thinking, feeling, acting human
being.**'(18)

Coda

So, what shall we do? I hear you cry!
I say go forward, not backward, make use of every new way
Every new technological advancement
Yet remember the body, the human body, your body
    As you tap and type, peer and squint at your screens,
    At your WAP enabled miniatures

Yes, the web holds virtually all you need...to read
But not all you really need... to experience
Ensure learners touch, taste, view, smell, hear objects of life
Make these environmental interactions requirements

Yes, celebrate that your phone may enable you to SEE
The body of the person to whom you speak
    Roll on video conferencing, web cams and clips
Learning experiences need to include people and interaction
    To require feedback and 'feed forth' reliant upon observing
    And sensing, taking- in of the other as part of the task
Build in dialogue and interactive tasks rather than solo, techno
responses

Yes, we may want innovative ways of assessing learning
And proof that learning has occurred
Yet our methods can never be fully future-proofed
We will need to remain vigilant to the way technology shapes
our bodies
And locate the body in the centre of the 'performance' of
knowledge

Penelope A Best PGCE, MCAT, SRDMT, senior arts therapies clinician, trainer, supervisor. Co-ordinator of new Polish Dance and Movement Psychotherapy training in Warsaw, core tutor on Rotterdam programme, visiting tutor in Slovenia. Honorary Research Fellow in School of Human Life Sciences, Roehampton University, and recent Visiting Research Fellow in Open Creativity Centre, Open University. CAPE mentor for teacher/ artist collaborations in creativity projects for national Creative Partnerships. Researcher and evaluator for educational projects on creativity (e.g. 2004/5: 'Creative Friend Model' for CP Black Country; 'Personalised Learning' for Sorrell Foundation; 'Image Conscious' arts project for Camden Arts Centre). Senior lecturer Dance Movement Therapy at Roehampton University. Private supervision practice ('Moment to Moment'). Publishes and presents regularly at international conferences.

Reference

1 Barrow, J. (1995) The Artful Universe.
Oxford: Clarendon Press.

2 Best P. (2003). Interactional Shaping within Therapeutic
Encounters.
USA Body Psychotherapy Journal, 2.2, pp.26 – 44

3 Gardner, H. (1999) Intelligences Reframed: Multiple
intelligences for the 21st century. *New York: Basic Books*

4 O'Conner, J. & McDermott, I. (1996) Principles of NLP.
London: *Thorsons*

5 Barrow, J. (1995) The Artful Universe. Oxford:
Clarendon Press.

6 Parker, G. & Best, P. (2004) Reflecting processes and
shifting positions in dance movement therapy. Moving On.
Dance Therapy Association of Australia 3.3. pp 2-4

7 Parker & Best *(Ibid)*

8 Massey, D. (1999) Spaces of politics. In Massey, D., Allen,
J., & Sarre, P. (eds.) Human Geography *Today, pp. 279 -294.
Cambridge: Polity*

9 Lawley, J. & Tompkins, P. (2000) Metaphors in Mind:
Transformation through symbolic modeling. London: *The
Developing Company Press*

10 Moore, C. & Yamamoto, K. (1988) Beyond Words:
Movement observation and analysis. *Philadelphia: Gordon &
Breach*

11 Winnicott, D.W. (1965).   The maturational process
and the facilitating environment. New York: *International
Universities Press.*

12 Moore, C. & Yamamoto, K. (1988) Beyond Words: Movement observation and analysis. Philadelphia: *Gordon & Breach*

13 Csordas, T.J. (1999). Embodiment and cultural phenomenology. In Weiss, G. & Haber, H.F. (Eds.). Perspectives on Embodiment : The intersections of nature and culture New York: *Routledge*

14 Moon, J. (2002) A Handbook of reflective and Experiential Learning: Theory and practice. *Routledge Falmer: London*

15 Bresler, L. (ed). (2004) Knowing Bodies, Moving Minds: towards embodied teaching and learning. *Dordrecht, Netherlands: Kluwer*

16 Bartenieff , I. (1980) Body Movement: coping with the environment New York : *Gordon & Breach*

17 Bateson, G. (1972) Steps to an Ecology of Mind. New York: *Ballantine Books.*

18 Bartenieff , I. *(ibid)*

VILLAGE SOUP - SOME OLD IDEAS MIXED DIFFERENTLY

John Alexander

Introduction

It has been more than forty years since I attended school. I was involved in my son's education about fifteen years ago. The only real contact was through the PTA, my son's friends and after-school activities. He did well at school and won a scholarship to Oxford. The system has served us well.

However, as I have reflected on the system and what it produces, I have concluded there must be a better way.

As a preparation, I did a personal brainstorming session. I felt the need to generate a lot of ideas without evaluation and then with those ideas in the back of my mind, talk to some people who are currently involved in the system. I talked to some 14 and 15 year olds in school (who seemed to be interested in every thing but school!), a recently retired history teacher from an inner London school and a Professor of Education – a diverse group, selected opportunistically, in no way a representative sample, yet a good sounding-board/reality check for my ideas.

Personal Brainstorm

So just suppose we had to invent an education system for this century, what would it look like? Here are the goals and wishes I generated in my personal brainstorming session:

1. I wish all parents were involved in the development of the curriculum and all aspects of children's education
2. How to change the political situation in each school
3. Wish there was no tenure and payment of educators would be based on results
4. Discipline of a child would involve discipline of a parent because the parent is responsible for the child's behaviour

5. How to go back to the principle of a one-room schoolhouse
6. Technology for communication would be built into the system
7. Every child would have to be apprenticed during the school term and learn life skills alongside adults, doing work in their daily lives.
8. Children would be paid to go to school; if they did not achieve certain results, they could be fired
9. How to mix the ingredients differently
10. Wish parents would be involved on a daily basis
11. Wish teachers did not have to care about their careers
12. Wish there was no tenure
13. Wish schools would teach life skills
14. Wish each child had highly educated and motivated parents
15. Wish schools were not just for child minding
16. Wish schools were fun for the parents
17. Wish they were fun for the children
18. Wish they would concentrate just on the basics
19. Wish everything that was basic had to involve the parents
20. How to re educate parents where needed
21. Wish money for education was never a problem
22. Wish all schools were small schools
23. Wish there could not be schools, as we know them
24. How to get rid of all the real estate
25. How to have children teach each younger kids
26. Wish kids could wake up smart
27. Wish education were a life long exercise for all
28. How do we train people to teach
29. Wish it could all take place at home
30. Wish all children could read and write before they attend a school
31. Wish to agree about what the school is teaching
32. Wish to separate life skills from education and sport and music and art
33. How to be certain about what a person needs to function and do well in society

Talking To The Users

My next step was to talk to some kids and check out my ideas, see if I could develop them a little and give them some meaning.

What a shock! The dozen or so fourteen and fifteen year olds that I spoke to were surly, could hardly comprehend the questions I was asking, shuffled their feet, looked scruffy and hardly had an idea between them. They were a very small sample of what education is producing, but my instincts tell me they represent a good many kids of their age. I mentioned this to a teacher at the school and her response was that I should talk to a different class, a class who were more 'with it'. And that is probably one of the things wrong with the system. People are left behind. Because everyone cannot be first, the system seems to be designed for failure. This seems to be a fact of life, reinforced by streaming, tests and exams to find out who the winners are.

Why, I wonder, were the kids I met so uninspired? Was I the same at their age? It is hard to remember. They told me they liked school only when it gave them a chance to meet with friends. They liked the science class so long as there were physical experiments. They also liked activities in which kids were allowed to mix with all ages, not just their peers. They did not like the discipline process. I do not think they really know what discipline is. Teachers' hands are tied, and the students are handled with kid gloves. Not that I am in favour of physical punishment by teachers. However, there has to be a way to get their attention.

They did not like being told what to do, being controlled by school and the attitude of the teachers. It seemed to me that at some level they were ready for a whole lot more responsibility and self-direction, although I do not think they would see it that way. They were way too cool to be concerned about anything other than music and the opposite sex.

Next, I to talked to some teachers.

Conversation with Pete

I talked about ideas for this chapter with friends, and some teachers in a local service club. One particular conversation, with a recently retired history teacher from an inner London school, generated a spirited discussion and a lot of ideas.

Pete has spent his whole life teaching. It has been a passion for him and now he is retired he still works part time at a local school. No matter how I tried, I could not get him to talk about the education system per se; all his thoughts were curriculum based. No surprise I suppose. One of the underlying assumptions of this book is that if you are part of the system it is very hard to see how to change it. However, he had good ideas and was moved to email his thoughts to me a couple of days later – here they are.

1) Active learning not passive. Teacher needs to be a guide and facilitator rather than source of all knowledge.
2) Use of higher order questioning - open questions that have no set answers not closed questions, e.g. is our quality of life better than that of our grandparents?
3) Simulations and role-play such as mock elections.
4) Problem solving situations involving teamwork e.g. constructing a bridge out of newspaper to support a kilo or more
5) Mini-enterprises where groups set up businesses, manufacture or provide services and assess their performance. Closely linked with reality
6) Micro society - where kids set up a society, decide on the type of government, what qualities leaders should have and how decisions are made. The needs of the society are decided and individuals appointed in various roles e.g. farmers to produce food, carpenters to build homes etc. Decisions such as rewards have to be decided and value questions discussed e.g. should a nurse be better paid than a lawyer? Are all people equally valuable or should some groups be given greater rewards because they are more important to society? What should happen to those who break the rules? How should the wealth be spent?

7) Use of drama with all age groups is a great way to develop confidence and reveal hidden talents and abilities.

And then he said, "Of course many of these things are already happening in the best schools but not in most. Computers have revolutionised the way kids work but not necessarily the way they think. As teachers become more computer literate, they need to utilise the potential more productively and imaginatively in a cross-curricular approach.

There are some great things happening in schools in England, but narrow SAT scores can dominate, and the broader needs of children are not met. We all agree that children need literacy, numeracy, speaking, listening and I.T. skills. However, the challenge is to teach them in an imaginative and not a didactic way".

I tend to agree with him.

How do we get teachers to think differently and to stop reinforcing inappropriate and outdated paradigms? Within the existing system it is probably very difficult to help kids to think differently because the teachers are so much a part of the system and what is the point of giving them technology to use if it only reinforces existing ways of thinking?

A Chance Meeting

Then, by chance, I met a professor of education. She was excited to hear about the idea of this book and we began to discuss and share our thinking. We agreed that the parents have to be more involved. I mentioned that I was beginning to play around with the idea of how we could recreate the benefits of the one room schoolhouse, using modern technology. She loved the idea especially the way in which it causes mixed age levels to take more responsibility for helping each other.

As we talked more about the idea we explored what should be taught. It is easy to say reading, writing, math, and science. But if you take reading and writing do you also include literature, creative writing, penmanship, etc. The same applies to math and science and where do you draw the line?

The discussion once again revolved around the curriculum. I eventually got on to the idea of how teachers are paid. I proposed that the government should legislate pay for teachers pegged to and at a level equal to what we pay our politicians. Understandably that was a well-received idea.

I do think teachers are hopelessly underpaid. If we really value what they do it needs to be reflected in the pay scales. Serious improvements in salary, I believe, are an absolute must.

We agreed the local community should have to come up with the money. It should not automatically come from increased taxes. Funds that are currently in the system could be re-directed, applied in a different way. I do not know the exact details. However, if we get rid of all that exists in the current system of education, we would have funds to be used in new ways.

We explored the idea of payment of teachers by results. She flatly rejected the idea because it creates and reinforces the need to use exams to establish the value a teacher creates, and a reflection of how they do their job.

However, I disagreed with her. I believe she was making assumptions and was trapped by existing paradigms. As I listened to her, I found myself wishing there was a way to evaluate a teacher's performance on the job without subjecting the students to performing the job evaluation through their achievement in an exam. However, I am stuck and do not yet see a way. It is just another problem to solve!

I am not against testing of students per se. I do dislike them being used to evaluate a teacher's worth. Also, I dislike the effect of test results on the assumptions a teacher makes about the student. John Holt, in "How Children Fail" and "How Children Learn" (first published in the Sixties) showed how teachers' behaviour is clearly changed in a negative way towards students who apparently scored low in test results.

We talked about an idea of education clubs and the involvement of the community to set the curriculum and standards and how this would be organised on a local and national level. She pointed out that a lot of this exists but could do with improvement and more community based activity. It was hard to get our minds away from what currently exists and difficult to see how to change both the practical and political aspects.

Whether we agreed on the details or not, did not really matter. We did agree that participation of parents was critical and wondered just how many parents know what is in their kids' school bags when they come home at night. Do the parents really know what their kids were doing at school today? We did not think so!

Is education the right of every child?

In one final brief discussion, she said, "public education is an entitlement of every child". This stopped me in my tracks. It sounded right at first but since then I have wondered. Is it really? It is certainly desirable. I can't imagine that anyone in the world would wish to deny a child, or an adult if it comes to that, an education. Is it a right, an entitlement?

I think it is not an inalienable right, as in the American Constitution where it is stated that every American has the right to life, liberty and the pursuit of happiness.

Our children are not entitled to an education because of who they are. Of course civilised society wants to educate itself; it is the key to our future. Our parents and grandparents earned the right through political protest, social pressure and a lot of hard work. The right to a public education has been earned and paid for. It is available because of the work of those that came before us. And, how terrible would it be if we squandered the work of our recent ancestors by neglecting something worked so hard for and hard won.

How do we make our children, and many parents, understand their responsibility to use the public education system; to nurture it and help it to continue to grow and be strong. If we neglect and/or consider it an entitlement that somebody else will provide, it will, more and more, give way to private education where only those that can afford it will get it.

The public education system needs to be more about creating the right environment, social and political, in which a person can function and pursue their educational needs and desires. It is up to the individual, the parents and the users of public education to get what they want from the system through active participation in the process.

Following all this talk with other people and with myself, I narrowed my ideas down to six strategies.

1. Legislate for and educate parental involvement

Improve the way parents are involved and make it a necessity. I am not sure how much and what kind of involvement of parents is needed. On balance, though, it has to be a whole lot more than it is currently. Parents need to be involved, at a local level, in the development of the curriculum, selection of teachers, how they are paid, where the money to pay for them comes from. They need to know and understand what their children do everyday at school. And they need to find ways to help their children understand that an education is something that their grandparents and great grandparents worked hard for. Parents have to be brought into the schools more. It has to become mandatory.

If a child is misbehaving at school, it must be dealt with in a way that puts the responsibility on the parents. There is no point in punishing a child when the values taught in the classroom are undermined by what happens at home. In my more radical moments, I think parents should be fined for their children's poor behaviour, lack of attendance etc.

2. Change the way teachers are paid

Obviously the issue is complicated and this thought experiment does not resolve it. So here are a few wishes:
* No performance related pay where part of that performance is exam results.
* Pay teachers the same as we pay our politicians. The money could be available; after all, consider what we are spending on our military around the world.
* Change the control and management of education funds and put it all in local hands.
* Get rid of the national and central organisation and by doing so change the political power in the system. If the way teachers are paid changes, the power structure and decision making is changed and the system will change,

3. Sell all the real estate. Develop virtual one-room schoolhouses

Get rid of all the real estate and associated expenses. Have every community develop a virtual one-room schoolhouse. This could possibly be a small group of mixed ages communicating electronically and meeting on a regular basis in a private house, town office, hotel or any other location where they would have access to the technology they need to help them achieve their education goals. Each group would have a teacher who has any number of groups he or she works with. By using technology the teacher could work with all the groups at the same time for a particular period and then work with individual groups according to the learning objectives.

One of the priorities would be learning how to learn. Modern technology puts masses of information at our fingertips. Learning how to use the information is an important part of the process. With good learning skills, we could return to the virtual one room school house as many times as we wish throughout our lives as new learning becomes important to us.

4. Create local learning clubs

These would be an extension of the virtual one-room schoolhouses. Parents would have to join together in the community to make this happen. The age groups would be mixed. Older kids would be able to help the younger ones, and visa-versa. Everyone would have to do his or her share. If you have a child in the system, it becomes your civic responsibility to be involved in these clubs.

5. Pay teenagers for civic service before higher education

The pay would be in return for two years of civic service, between senior school and university. It would be a bit like conscription used to be. Civic service would be for four days a week with the fifth working day exploring different education tracks that one could take in the future. The money earned in civic service would partially, or wholly, be used to pay for each person's university level education.

6. Use retired professionals as teachers

What a terrible waste and a lost opportunity not to use people with a lifetime of experience and knowledge. Let retirees into the classroom as helpers, teachers and coaches both to the students and teachers. Have them involved in the management of the school, which frees up the teachers for the classrooms. Have the retirees tell stories of their past and bring recent history to life, allowing our children to see the recent past through the eyes of people that were there.

We have a growing army of seniors who are healthy and active. For many it would be a good opportunity and a pleasure to help. They could receive some pay and benefits. It need not be at the level needed by younger people with growing families. I think it could be a win both for the students and for the seniors who, in the September of their years, would be pleased to be helping.

Conclusion

These six concepts are only a convenience. It could be that within the ideas in the chapter are a germ of a concept that will spark an imagination somewhere leading to useful, if not radical change

I wish my ideas were more radical. As I started out on this thought experiment, I had hoped to come up with something that would strike fear into the heart of those currently in control of the system and excitement in those who clearly see the problems and would dearly love to see more change. However, you never know. The creative process is messy and untidy. If enough people kick enough ideas around some of them will no doubt evolve into useful new directions. The challenge for those in the system is to be prepared to play with and find value in ideas that at first do not seem feasible.

John Alexander was born in London, England and has lived in the USA for the past eleven years as an escapee from corporate life. He currently divides his time between the mid coast of Maine in the summer, where he owns two RV parks and Key West Florida, in the winter, where most days he sails in the warm waters of the Gulf of Mexico.

From 1974 to 1994 he worked as a consultant for Synectics Inc. From 1989 to 1994 he was the managing partner in the UK. Synectics Inc.'s focus during that period was the development of creative and strategic thinking in organisations. John was both a teacher of the creative process and facilitator, helping people to work together to develop new ideas, products and processes.

TECHNOLOGY EDUCATION FOR THE FUTURE

Dr. Gill Hope

Introduction

Design and Technology was introduced as a school subject for all children in the UK under the 1988 Education Act. Its content emerged from trends within secondary schools, combined with the views of vocal industrialists and the desire of government to increase the British GNP. Despite "Design and Technology" being a cumbersome subject title, many have, rightly, fought hard to keep the design side alive. It is not just vocational training. It is teaching children that they too can have good ideas and make choices about products that they want to make or have made by others.

Design and Technology education is vital for children growing up in an age that is increasingly technology-dependent. Design, like education, is future-oriented and human civilization is technologically designed. We dare not provide an education bounded in a world-view that is fast being superceded by new realities. We should constantly reflect on the philosophical underpinnings of education and the assumptions to which we are working. We need to ensure that they are relevant to the future as well as to today and help us to equip young people for the ever-changing world that will become tomorrow.

At the chalk face

Design and Technology (as every child's entitlement) was launched on the unsuspecting British educational public without a clear definition of what the subject *was*. Essential underlying questions had not been addressed: What was its rationale, its knowledge base, its underlying philosophy? What were its meta-skills to be? What were their contributory skills and knowledge? How do cognitive and practical aspects build together into the education of the skilled Design-and-technologist?

After the introduction of the National Curriculum, it became obvious, in journals, articles and conference proceedings, that research into how young children learn had transformed itself into how they could best be taught the National Curriculum. I remember walking down the path to my classroom thinking to myself "Research is dead then." Prior to the National Curriculum, there was little research into how small children designed things that they made, yet after its introduction, books and articles appeared to instruct teachers how to teach them to do so. The National Curriculum became the benchmark against which to measure capability and progress towards being good at Design and Technology. The lack of clarity about what this new subject actually entailed, especially since it was couched in unfamiliar jargon, led to confusion and distrust of the subject among Primary school teachers. As a result, Design and Technology were squeezed out the back door as soon as greater emphasis on Literacy, Numeracy and ICT was heralded in through the front door.

If we wish to go on a search for a philosophy for the future of Design and Technology education, we need to be sure that all our stakeholders, if not coming with us, are at least happy for us to take the journey. Our new paradigm (Kuhn, 1962), should we locate it, will affect teaching and learning at the most fundamental level: what counts as knowledge and how it is transmitted and acquired, as well as the way we organize resources, timetables, assessment - in short, our aims, objectives, success criteria, experiences of pupils and evaluation of the results.

Whatever our new paradigm looks like, it must address the needs of children to be children. Children are here and now creatures. We cannot teach them on an "eat up your greens, they will make you grow strong" basis. Children still prefer the taste of chocolate. Fortunately, when questioned, most children say they enjoy Design and Technology lessons. They enjoy hands-on problem solving, the freedom to discuss, try out, make things which they have imagined and invented.

Designing for technology

The valuing of science above other ways of truth-knowing, and the economic need for more engineers, led to technology being firmly coupled to the empirical model of knowledge (the advertising industry contributed the catchphrase "the appliance of science"). However, the appliance of science is not the same as the creation of science, and is certainly only a small part of design, which is concerned, not with the search for defining generalizations, but with finding a specific workable solution to an often poorly defined problem.

Ryle (1949) divided knowledge into *knowing how* and *knowing that*, from which I have developed my own theory of how Design and Technology knowledge works:

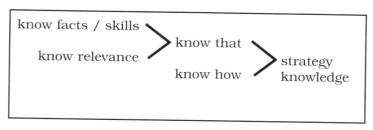

This extends Ryle's *knowing that* to cover technical knowledge and skills, recognition of similarities to other situations and even analogical flights of imagination, as well as factual information. Polanyi (1958) coined the phrase *tacit knowledge*, which is pre-articulate and includes hand-skills, hunches, creativity and inner feelings of rightness. Traditionally, education has devalued this means of knowing. So our new paradigm must re-assert the importance of the heuristic, coupled with social responsibility, to which Polanyi devotes a whole chapter (Ch.7 "Conviviality") in his book "Personal Knowledge".

However, knowing some facts or having some skills is not all that is needed to solve a problem. The problem-solver needs to know which information can be harnessed to the solving of the current problem - i.e. *knowing relevance* to the current situation. *Know how* is needed to turn this into the strategy for solving the problem. This combination of *know that, know relevance* and *know how* form the basis of the strategy to be employed to solve the problem. The choice of appropriate strategy in any problem-solving situation depends on the depth and salience of the *know that* and *know how* which support it.

In discussing designing with children, this can be reduced to three basic questions:
What do you know / can you do?
How does that apply to this problem / what else might apply?
How will you use that knowledge / skill to solve this problem?

In "The Construction of Knowledge", Von Glasenfeld asserted that knowledge can never be interpreted as a picture that *matches* the real world (like paint matches some already on the wall), but only as a key that unlocks possible pathways for us. Many keys fit the same lock (knowledge exploited by burglars!) and in looking for design solutions there are frequently several possible right answers.

A changing world

By the nature of its subject matter, Design and Technology, is a continually and fast-changing field, requiring a paradigm of teaching and learning which fits its recipients for a future of rapid and possibly radical change. The sweeping changes wrought by the microchip revolution are just a foretaste of the depth and breadth of the changes that the children in our schools today will experience in their lifetime. Whatever paradigm we accept and promote, *change* needs to be part of it - to be celebrated, created, relished and sustained, not merely "coped with".

It is surely a contradiction to hold a backward-looking, conventional view of a subject that involves children planning their own future actions within each activity or project. Inherent in any new paradigm for Design and Technology, therefore, must be an awareness of future-orientated issues. We should not, therefore, aim to equip children for such a rapidly changing job-market by introducing them to the new technologies in school workshops. The rate of change is too fast to build a curriculum on any specific technology (Toffler 1970). Despite the rhetoric about people's future as never before depending on their education, education itself is backward-looking, bent on "cranking out Industrial Man - people tooled for survival in a system that will be dead before they are." The curriculum, Toffler claimed, "is not based on … any understanding of what skills Johnny will require to live in the hurricane's eye of change."

The most certain thing about the future is *change*, rapid and continuous. The most important resource in the face of rapid technological and economic change is the capacity of companies and individuals for creativity, innovation, flexibility and adaptability. These are generic capabilities which Design and Technology education should foster and develop in our pupils.

Creative designing

Inventors and designers are highly creative individuals and creativity seems to be one of the most elusive of human qualities. Where does it come from? How do we recognise it in small children? How can we foster it in the general school population?

A good phrase for creativity is Craft's (2000) *"possibility thinking"* or *"as if"* thinking. In a college workshop recently I came across the phrase *"dream room thinking"*. In re-thinking Design and Technology this has a double application. Not only am I indulging in "dream room thinking" myself, creating a personal wish list for an educative experience in a subject area about which I care passionately, but I perceive the subject itself as essentially to do with encouraging "dream room thinking" in others.

If Design and Technology as a mode of knowing can teach

anything to other areas of expertise and knowledge, it is in the acceptance of multiple solutions. The obsession with the search for *the theory of everything* has led science to *a theory of multiple universes.* The reaction against *the theory of intelligence* has led to *a theory of multiple intelligences.* In a world of increasingly complex and difficult socio-technological problems, we need not just the recognition of the *possibility of multiple solutions,* but to celebrate diversity and complexity as a strength, rather than yet another problem to be solved. Design and Technology is not just "good" for children because it will enable them to become creative at some future time and in some unknown workplace but because it fosters their creativity and playfulness *where they are now.*

There are management issues here, of course. How does a National Curriculum manage creativity and diversity? Is creativity really untamable and is it diametrically opposed to management? If we manage Design, will it cease to be creative? Creativity certainly does not thrive in tightly constrained methodologies. It is aware of too many other things. It can balance conflict on its nose and juggle with confusion at the same time. It can see structure in chaos storms and view rainbows in a grain of sand. Consistent with Heisenberg's uncertainty principle, stardust disappears under inspection. If we are designing a curriculum for designers and inventors, we should not try to catch this will o' the wisp and put it in a document labeled "moonshine" (and wait for it to fade). We must give freedom to our educators to foster the latent talents of our young people and trust them to find their own truth-way.

"All design is goal directed play" is the wonderful opening statement of Papanek's (1995) *"The Green Imperative"* that, perhaps, gives us a way into combining the pre-determined with the spontaneous. Play and creativity are fused in the fun and joy of young children and yet our adult-led model of teaching barely taps into these natural learning styles. We need to celebrate, not denigrate, children's play-learning and build on its strengths, its natural slipping and sliding of concepts into one another, fusing reality and fantasy, adapting found objects for another purpose. It can construct solutions from a single creative spark of an idea, maintain narrative in fantasy space across hours and days, and take other participants along for the ride. It involves team-building, disseminating ideas and accepting the ideas and enthusiasms of others, negotiating, accommodating and having a natural intuition for the rightness of fit in the context of the jointly created fantasy world.

To design a curriculum based on such intangibles, or build for a creative future, when no one knows or can predict what the future might hold, is not incompatible with a new paradigm for Design and Technology that could combine the flight of imagination with the reality of the problem to be solved. It just requires the abandonment of the pre-determined 'one right answer'.

Reflective designing

Human life is inherently value-laden and every corner of it, the intellectual equally with the affective, is permeated with our values. If design is in response to human need then it cannot duck the moral issue. Design education must embrace the difficult and frequently contradictory mess of ethics and responsibility. It should also contribute towards the spiritual dimension of personal development: the sense of wonder at, for example, the beauty of inlaid furniture or blown glass pieces that are almost art objects in their own right, or the sense of awe on entering a temple or cathedral - a man-made place that has been designed to enhance our sense of the numinous.

This respectful awareness of the process of creation, as well as admiration for the product itself, should become a central part of viewing and handling existing products as a stimulus for children's own work. This is a far more positive and enhancing response than "dis-assembly of made products", which haunts the backwoods of Design and Technology.

A corollary to that is the sense of achievement of producing something aesthetically pleasing oneself. An instrumentalist view of education as preparation for adult working life excludes those who have no such future. Designing as a creative experience, and making things as empowerment, as personal fulfilment, adding to the joy of life, are essential for those whose participation in society is limited by other difficulties. I treasure the memory and the small gifts created by two of my pupils who, through illness, never lived beyond their childhood years. Children in wheelchairs, who have to depend on the help of others to do things the rest of us take for granted, need to design and create, not just to feel in control, but to feel able to contribute.

By juxtaposing the development of self-esteem and pride in creation with reflection on the made world and the relationship between it and the natural resources of the planet, the issues which Design and Technology address become big and bold and central to the education of all. This to me is the direction in which technology education should go. It takes hold of the spiritual dimension of creativity in one hand and the social responsibility embedded in citizenship education in the other. It is also a view founded on the needs of *children*, regardless of their future contribution to the economic state of the nation.

In a world of increasing globalisation, we need to succour the traditions of the marginalised. Western technology has proved itself short of answers on many issues. Especially for older children, issues of sustainability, environmental damage, social change, economics and moral and ethical implications need to be added to the mix. These issues need airing in our technology curriculum, not left to P.S.H.E. and R.E. to provide the only alternative (and possibly critical) voice in the wilderness. We need to include the insights inherent in non-Western technological traditions and to embrace the issues of cultural and environmental responsibility by encouraging pupils to examine products for sustainability as well as fitness for purpose, to endorse the personal creativity of each individual and to educate for responsibility to society, to the environment and to the safety of the planet.

Towards a new future for technology education

In order to develop technology education for the future, we need first to clarify our philosophy of education and be upfront about the difficulty of such a task, accepting help from a wide forum, especially practising teachers. We need to recognize the diversity of opinion and see at least part of our task as fostering creative, divergent thinking. We need desperately to know *what else works*.

Our new paradigm needs to be socially responsive and educate for reflective consumerism, in the global and environmental sense, not just the narrow, market-place sense of the term. It needs to meet the present needs of *all* children, not just prepare those who will contribute most positively to the economic status of the nation. It must encourage children's self-esteem through creating pleasing solutions to specific problems, which will enable them to appreciate the solutions of others, both the creations of their peers and in the made environment. It must teach them to discuss the morality of technology, the concept of "progress", and learn to address more than just the client's needs. By aiming to address the big issues, ethical, social and environmental, whilst trying to solve the specific and particular, Design and Technology can provide a forum for discussion and reflection which contributes towards education for responsible citizenship

Finally, a new paradigm must not be prescriptive. It must recognize the creativity and dynamism of designing. In teaching children the rules of the game, it must also give them the freedom to explore bending and breaking the mould. This will only occur in classrooms where the teacher is not constrained, otherwise we shall continue to lose our most reflective, creative and innovative practitioners to careers in which their most precious talents are encouraged rather than ignored.

It would be a pleasing irony if the subject most lauded by politicians for its instrumentalism and vocationalism and contribution to the country's GNP, were instead to lead the way forward on the education of the spiritual, moral and social dimensions of what it is to be human. But then technology has always been a leader, a creative force in human development.

113

The distinction between humanity and our closest primate relatives is in our ability to reflect and make choices. Our greatest contribution to the technological possibilities of the future will be to educate those to whom we are entrusting our future to make creative and responsible design choices with regard to the technology by which they are surrounded.

Dr. Gill Hope is a Senior Lecturer in Design and Technology Education at Canterbury Christ Church University College, Kent, UK. Her research interests focus on the development of young children's design skills. She is a regular contributor of journal articles and conferences papers on aspects of Design and Technology education. This article is based on a paper given at the Design and Technology Association Conference 2002.

References

Craft, A. (2000) *Creativity across the Primary Curriculum: Framing & Developing Practice*; London; Routledge

Kuhn, T.S. (1962) *The Structure of Scientific Revolutions*; Chicago; The University of Chicago Press

Papanek, V. (1995) *The Green Imperative: Ecology and Ethics in Design and Architecture*; London; Thames & Hudson

Polanyi, M. (1958) *Personal Knowledge: Towards a Post-Critical Philosophy*; London; Routledge

Ryle, G. (1949) *The Concept of Mind*; London; Hutchinson

Toffler, A. (1970) *Future Shock*; London; Pan Books

Von Glasenfeld, E. (1987) *The Construction of Knowledge*; Seaside, California; Intersystems Publications

RESHAPING UK EDUCATION

Marilyn Fryer and Caroline Fryer

Introduction

It's rare to be asked what you would like the future of education to be, but why should this be rare? Why don't we spend more time thinking freely about what *might be?* After all, we know that we have to imagine our future before we can create it. We don't spend nearly enough time doing that, yet the future is where we're all going to spend the rest of our lives!

One way to seek answers to this huge but intriguing question is to ask even more questions such as, '*What does education involve? What is it for? Who is it for? Where should it be delivered? When and how will it be delivered?*' Questions such as these have bedevilled educationists for many years; college libraries are full of dusty tomes about them and students have long been bogged down in them. And this begs yet another question, which is '*Why after all this time and all this effort has a satisfactory answer not yet been found?*' This brings to mind the delightful, elderly economics lecturer who always set his students the same exam questions, because although the questions never change, the answers do.

Imagining education half a century ahead is not easy in a climate in which many organisations shy away from strategic planning even five years ahead. Indeed, when we asked a group of headteachers this question, their immediate reaction was that 50 years was much too far into the future to even contemplate.

But is the future of education really so unpredictable? True we've moved from the machine age to the information age, and the current education system is still struggling to catch up. Yet, in contrast to the proliferation of information and the increased speed of communication, human development hasn't moved forward all that much. This is hardly surprising since it operates on an evolutionary rather than revolutionary timescale.

Future education needs to address human development in the context of significant technological and social change. So, ideally education needs to optimise all aspects of individuals' development, allowing children and young people to gradually gain independence as they mature and become increasingly able to make their own choices. Logically, this would mean taking systematic account of emotional, social and physical and cognitive development at every stage of life. However, this is a tall order and unlikely to ever be fully achieved. Paradoxically, this would be good, since healthy neglect is more likely to produce psychologically healthy individuals than over-solicitousness. In other words, it is possible to strive so hard to create the 'perfect' education system that what you are trying to create gets destroyed. To take an analogy from social work, a key aim is that parents do a 'good enough' job of bringing up their children, not a 'perfect' one. Arguably the same applies to education. At present, formal UK education places greatest emphasis on intellectual development with social, physical and emotional development trailing behind, so there is plenty of scope to create a better balance, if not a 'perfect' one.

What is 'education'?

Definitions of education are legion and we have no intention of cycling through them all here, except to note that the term 'education' comes from the Latin 'educere' to lead out – implying the need for an educator. But of course the definition of 'learning' is equally relevant to human development. The most frequently quoted one (at least in psychological circles) is 'Learning is a change in behaviour as a result of experience,' normally attributed to Gordon Allport. This definition allows for the fact that learning can (and does) happen anywhere. It often happens without the learner even being aware that learning is occurring. Learning may be helpful or maladaptive. And now we have yet another dilemma: *How much should future education involve teaching and how much learning?*

Mindful that experience teaches our bad flute players as well as our good ones (Plato) and that taking the middle road is normally the best strategy, we favour a balanced approach to future education. This involves a combination of teacher-led education and pupil/student-led learning. Very young children, propelled by curiosity, are excellent at learning for themselves. But for effective learning, sooner or later there needs to be an enabler - someone who has the learner's best interests at heart and can arrange the learning situation to suit (including knowing when to stand back and avoid interfering).

Interestingly, our research has shown that what bests distinguishes highly creative teachers from those less creative is the importance the highly creative teachers attach to taking students' learning needs into account (Fryer, 1996).

What and who is future education for?

Any educational provision needs to be primarily for the benefit of individual learners, so as to enable people to live happy and fulfilling lives. At the same time, there needs to be some benefit for society. From a developmental perspective, future educational provision needs to be accessible to people of all ages. There could be some mixed-age learning provision to allow young and older people to learn from one another, for example. But there would also need to be plenty of opportunities for same-age group activities. This would ensure that the learning needs of any particular age group were catered for and help young people especially to develop a clear sense of identity.

What will the focus of future education be?

The focus would be on the many different aspects and 'stages' of human development in the context of the modern world and our diverse society. But, crucially, it would ensure that developing learners' creativity was high on the agenda so as to equip learners for both the present and the future. It was the realisation that key aspects of human development were being ignored in much formal education (plus the fact that many children were bored at school) which sparked our interest in creativity and led to the establishment of The Creativity Centre in 1998. By *creative* we don't just mean generating ideas, but rather the ability to progress as far as possible and invent one's future.

If we adopt this broad definition of creativity, then a great deal of what is currently in the curriculum may be subsumed under a creative education, rather than the reverse. Creativity is not, in our view, an 'add on' but rather the culmination of individual knowledge, skills and motivation. So, in order to create our future, we will need an education system which equips us with the capacity to be creative, provides relevant knowledge and skills, is exciting and fulfilling and is delivered in age-appropriate ways.

Core literacy, numeracy and investigative skills will still be crucial, but there is a need for more effective delivery. A greater emphasis could usefully be put on life skills, self-sufficiency, survival, human relations and other skills. Also, it makes sense to offer opportunities for learners to sample a whole array of learning options (these could include traditional subjects such as foreign languages, geography, history, the arts, as well as subjects not yet invented). Physical education could include play, sports and physical exercise and would be made available on a daily basis. It could also include activities in the areas of health and nutrition. Healthy emotional development normally begins with the development of secure bonds between parent (or carer) and infant. The gradual development of good self esteem and self image can be supported in educational settings, as can the development of clear self identities and independence. There are, however, many different influences at work and no educational provision can deal with all the issues. Nevertheless, there is much that can be done to support healthy emotional development.

In any educational provision, there needs to be increased opportunities for building better social relationships. This includes, for example, providing greater opportunities for learning through social play for young children, challenging projects requiring group co-operation for young people, together with opportunities for other activities which encourage collaboration and self awareness e.g. educational drama or environmental projects. Beyond this, better opportunities for young (and older) people to learn more about child development and human relationships could be provided.

Some aspects of cognitive development are already emphasised in education, but there is scope for far more emphasis on activities which require creative thinking. Future education will need to include applied opportunities for analogical thinking, scenario-building, individual and group problem solving, for example. This will help people to deal with novel situations and be proactive about the future. In parallel, there will need to be more emphasis on developing imaginative thinking through opportunities for imaginative play, reading fiction and listening to music, for instance. Individual working, at least some of the time, and opportunities for deep absorption in tasks which require creative thinking and which learners find fascinating also helps develop creative abilities, as discussed in Fryer (1996).

Where could it take place?

Valuable learning takes place in the course of every day life. From an early age, all aspects of human development benefit from play - a frequently under-rated means of learning. But although a certain amount of learning occurs in the home and in everyday life, we also need a broader range of opportunities.

A key issue here is how we learn. Future education needs to cater for all the different ways in which learning occurs. This includes being motivated by tasks which stimulate our curiosity, by the challenge of pitting our wits against our own past achievements and the influence of 'competence models' - people we admire and want to emulate - as well as other forms of reinforcement. In other words, to be effective, learning needs to take place in circumstances in which we are motivated to learn.

One scenario is to develop creative learning centres which offer greater scope for educational activities than are currently available, which are less prescriptive and more appealing; and which are complemented by opportunities for learning, discovery and adventure in the wider world. Such centres could provide links to projects and initiatives located elsewhere and act as a hub for access to a wide range of learning opportunities in a variety of settings.

Creative learning centres would not be so large as to be impersonal, and they would be constructed in such a way as to allow each group to build up a sense of belonging and develop their own identity. They would need to be imaginative, of high quality, well-maintained and attractive. Greater use could be made of the outdoors as well as the indoor environment. The outdoors could be used for all manner of learning including environmental projects, horticulture, science, construction and architecture, art and design, maths and literacy projects, for example.

How could it take place?

It is possible to envisage some sort of allocation system for the formal aspects of learning – each directed to a particular aspect of development and developmental age of the learner. The younger the child the greater likelihood that learning will take place close to home and in a smaller setting. Older children would be offered increased opportunities for exploration and challenge (with suitably-trained *enablers* on hand when necessary). There would still be some formal classes and direct teaching but also lots of opportunities for discovery, using a variety of media. There could still be core and optional courses for different groups. It would be up to each family or individual to manage their allocation and this would enable them to select the type of education they want, how it would be taught, when it would be delivered, by whom and where. Mentors and other advisors could be on hand to assist where necessary with regard to choices. 'Taster sessions' could be offered before final selections were made. There is an issue about the extent to which education should be compulsory.

Ideally, creative learning centres would be so exciting that no-one would want to miss out.

When should it happen?

Attendance at creative learning centres could be at flexible times, but for an agreed amount of time. There would also be opportunities to learn at home or in other venues instead. Ideally, the stage at which attendance would begin would depend on children's developmental age, as opposed to their chronological age, to cater for developmental variations. There would be no prescribed 'leaving date'. Instead, as they grew up, young people would be able to select more or less of the provision on offer depending on their circumstances, though the area where this was accessed could vary.

Who will make it happen?

As far as formal education goes, the initiative would need to be taken by the government or some independent body in which various checks and balances prevent excessive dominance by any single interest group and to ensure the health and safety of learners. This body would also need to take overall responsibility for funding, although this could come from a variety of sources. They would also decide on broad policy but within that there would be as much choice as possible.

Conclusion

Clearly this paper has only provided the briefest indication of how future education could look. A more detailed and considered plan would need to be mapped out for each age group and area, but we wouldn't necessarily have to start from scratch. Good practice and provision could be built on in ways which make learning more accessible, enjoyable and exciting for everyone, with more built-in choice and opportunity. Future learning would address a much wider range of developmental needs than are currently addressed and this would have a tremendous pay-off in terms of increased competences, a happier and more productive workforce, and healthier, more creative people, better able to lead satisfying and fulfiling lives and more able to direct the course of their lives. All this sounds pretty idealistic but, as argued earlier, creating any kind of 'perfect' solution could destroy the very thing we are trying to create. But if we succeed even in doing a 'good enough' job then many people's lives should be improved.

Marilyn Fryer BA (Hons) GradCertEd PhD C.Psychol AFBPsS FRSA is a Director of The Creativity Centre Ltd. She is a chartered psychologist and qualified teacher. Formerly Reader in Psychology at Leeds Metropolitan University, Marilyn has twenty years' experience of devising and delivering creativity development programmes at undergraduate and post-graduate levels. She specialises in creativity research and consultancy for national and international organisations, including government bodies. She has published and presented internationally in the USA, Europe and Asia. She is author of the book *Creative Teaching and Learning* and editor of the internationally authored book, *Creativity & Cultural Diversity*. She has written numerous book chapters, reports and articles in the academic and popular press.

Caroline Fryer, BA (Hons) PGDip is Chief Executive of The Creativity Centre Educational Trust and a Director of The Creativity Centre Ltd. Caroline specialises in creativity development and cultural diversity and undertakes research, consultancy and the production of learning materials. She runs the Centre's *Science Alliance* programme for teachers and young people and has extensive experience of devising and delivering creative educational programmes for educators and young people in this country and overseas. Her background is in the media and education. Caroline has developed creativity learning materials for university and organisational use. She has published in this country and the USA, is a UK Correspondent for Creativity's Global Correspondents, and has run a major international conference on *Creativity and Cultural Diversity*.

Reference

Fryer, M. (1996) *Creative Teaching and Learning*. London: Paul Chapman Publishing.

BEYOND MATERIALISTIC EDUCATION STEINER (WALDORF) EDUCATION FOR THE EVOLUTION OF HUMAN CONSCIOUSNESS

Richard House

'Materialistic learning... dominates education... Education has become an institution whose purpose... is not to make culture, not to serve the living cosmos, but to harness humankind to the dead forces of materialism. Education, as we know it, from pre-school through graduate school, damages the soul.'

Robert Sardello, Ph.D.

'It is of great importance to find an answer to the needs of our times through an education which is based on a real understanding of humankind's evolution.'

'If... mechanical thinking is carried into education,... there is no longer any natural gift for approaching the child himself. We experiment with the child because we can no longer approach his heart and soul.'

'It is inappropriate to work towards standardising human souls through future educational methods or school organisation.'

Rudolf Steiner

Introduction

'If in education we coerce the impulses of human nature, if we do not know how to leave this nature free, but wish to interfere on our own part, then we injure the organism of the child for the whole of its earthly life.'

Rudolf Steiner

I am all too aware of the ambitious nature of my chapter title. Yet I make no apology for the breadth of my chosen ground, nor for the boldness of my vision; for I believe that education systems in the Western world's era of 'Late Modernity' are demonstrably in abject crisis, even teetering on the brink of meltdown. As I write, late March 2005, for example, I am listening to distressing media reports on the burgeoning number of violent attacks by school pupils upon Britain's teachers. All of which makes it urgent that some 'clear-blue sky thinking' is pursued about the barrenness of our soullessly utilitarian education system. My central theme in what follows is that we have to consider what needs to be done – or what paradigms transcended - so that the education of our children can serve and take forward the mature evolution of human consciousness, rather than being yet another materialistic fetter upon it.

I believe that the educational critique and alternative given by Rudolf Steiner at the beginning of the last century is a profoundly human vision which is even more relevant to our current times than it was a century ago. Steiner (Waldorf) education is by far the largest independent educational movement in the world, with approaching one thousand schools and well over 1,500 Kindergartens across the globe in every continent and culture. Schools, moreover, which have often been built from scratch with little if any government assistance, and which therefore possess a quite unique inner fortitude (because of the enormous love and commitment through which a community of families has come together to build them).

There is no space here to give anything approaching an adequate description of the education in its full richness and majesty (a carefully chosen term). There exists a wealth of literature on Steiner education – including over 20 books written by Steiner himself, and a vast secondary literature, just some of which is listed with the references for this article on the SEI website www.excite-education.org. Rather, I will focus on several core themes which Steiner education directly addresses, and which are broadly symptomatic of the malaise from which modern schooling systems are characteristically suffering.

Modernity's Assault on the Very Being of the Child

'If... the teacher continues to overload [the child's] mind, he will induce certain symptoms of anxiety. And if... he still continues to cram the child with knowledge in the usual way, disturbances in the child's growing forces will manifest themselves. For this reason the teacher should have no hard and fast didactic system... Illnesses that appear in later life are often only the result of educational errors made in the very earliest years of childhood. This is why... education... must study the human being as a whole from birth until death.'

Rudolf Steiner

In our technocratic age, 'the definition of the child is made so precise that the imaginative freedom of the individual child is denied, [and] the child's freedom to play and explore is severely curtailed' (Block, 1997). The relentless incursion of imposed cognitive-intellectual learning at ever earlier ages is just one example of these pernicious trends – and this in the face of mounting international evidence that the 'too much too soon' educational ideology may be doing untold developmental harm to a generation of children (e.g. Elkind, 1989; House, 2004a).

Mainstream education seems to have lost touch with a deep understanding of the developmental needs of children, and is, rather, preoccupied with foisting on to children an adult-centric agenda which is both developmentally inappropriate and educationally unnecessary (House, 2000). We are increasingly reading media reports about how, for example, children are becoming bored and disaffected with learning at ages as young as 6 or 7; how the rates of mental ill-health in children are at record levels and relentlessly rising; and how Ritalin prescriptions are also soaring. In the latter case, our society treats as a medical illness what might well be children's *understandable* response to, and unwitting commentary on, our 'mad' educational culture (House, 2002-3). Young boys' learning in particular is suffering dramatically as they are being forced to 'sit still' for long periods in formal settings which are failing quite fundamentally to meet their developmental needs

(Goddard Blythe, 2004; cf. also Steve Biddulph, 1997).

The importance of imaginative play in child development has been emphasised by a host of prominent educationalists – Alan Block, Emerson, Froebel, Susan Isaacs, Winnicott, Vygotsky, and, of course, Rudolf Steiner himself. The experience of free, *unintruded-upon* play is an absolutely essential precondition for the development of both a well-rounded, emotionally mature personality, and for inculcating the qualities of creativity, self-motivation and the lifelong love of learning (House, 2002a). Carl Jung wrote that 'without playing with fantasy, no creative work has ever come to birth. The debt we owe to the play of the imagination is incalculable.'

The freedom of imagination is a delicate human quality that can all too easily be damaged – sometimes irreparably - by technocratic educational practices. For Block, 'to deny imagination is to deny the very creativity that makes self possible... To deny imagination is to instil hatred where should stem love and creativity.' Moreover, modern schooling 'establishes a dictatorship over the child in which reality is defined by the other. ...[T]he imagination... [is] denied for the predetermined outlines of the other. This violence denies the very existence of the individual child and denies that child all opportunity to learn.' And in the face of a system which 'banishes children... under a dense cover of rationalistic, abstract discourse about "cognition", "development", "achievement", etc.', it becomes 'impossible to hear the child's own voice', in the process 'dismissing the child's experience and... falsifying the actual lived experience of children' (Block, 1997).

I propose (with Block) doing away for ever with fixed, government-imposed curricula, universal normalising standards, and the intensive surveillance through which we discipline our children. 'Until we create an environment in which the child may use the educational establishment *to create him or her self*, until we serve only as a frame on which the canvas may appear in paint, we will continue to practice extreme violence upon the child, denying him/her growth, health, and experience.' (Block) No wonder that Professor Nikolas Rose remarked that 'Childhood is the most intensively governed sector of personal existence' (Rose, 1989). Those parents fortunate enough to be able to home-educate, or to send their children to a Steiner (Waldorf) or 'human-scale' school run along humanistic lines, are far more in a position to nurture their children's inherent love of learning (House, 2002b), not least through the protection of their children's developing senses and imagination.

The State's Pernicious Involvement in Education

'An education that has gradually been taken over by the State has deprived man of active striving; it has made him into a devoted member of the State structure. [From school age onwards] the State lays claim to the child and he is trained to fit the patterns of the State; he ceases to be a person and bears the stamp of the state.'

Rudolf Steiner

A growing number of mainstream critics is beginning to challenge the central controlling role of the State in children's education (e.g. Stephen, 2005). Recently, for example, Professor of Education Ted Wragg bemoans the state (!) of education in Britain: 'What is the point,' he asks, 'of having any kind of structure in education when the whole thing is run by the No 10 Policy Unit?' (Wragg, 2005). Wragg's typically piercing comment challenges the mentality that unquestioningly assumes that career politicians should control the education of the nation's children (cf. the essays in Prickett and Erskine-Hill, 2002).

Dr Martin Stephen, high master of St Paul's, London, writes that education is too important to be left in the hands of politicians: 'Education policy takes 10 or 15 years to come to fruition, and governments rarely have more than three years' (Stephen, 2005). Stephen goes on to advocate a standing commission upon which would be represented the universities, employers and parents, and which would make policy recommendations to government. Rudolf Steiner anticipated these difficulties many decades ago, advocating that we 'work towards an independent school system, making it free of the state so that the state does not even inspect schools. The activity of self-administered schools should arise purely from cultural needs.'

Children's *intrinsic* motivation is severely compromised, if not destroyed, under a pressure to reach and maintain externally defined and imposed 'standards'. When children are exposed to the pressure of such 'extrinsic motivation', and are *made* to learn, they inevitably lose autonomy and self-regulation. We should hardly be surprised that too many young people are today leaving school without an interest in anything they have been taught.

In an address given on 20th August 1919, in what has turned out to be a prophetic commentary on the relentless incursion of the State's influence on education, Rudolf Steiner said: 'The State will tell us... what results to aim for, and what the State prescribes will be bad. Its targets are the worst ones imaginable, yet it expects to get the best possible results. Today's politics work in the direction of regimentation, and it will go even further than this in its attempts to make people conform.' And elsewhere: "the important thing is that we do not rob teachers of their strengths of personality by forcing them to work within the confines of government regulations... In a state school, everything is strictly defined... everything is planned with exactitude. With us, everything depends on the free individuality of each single teacher... Classes are entrusted entirely to the individuality of the class teacher... what we seek to achieve must be achieved in the most varied of ways. *It is never a question of external regulations.*' (emphasis added)

Today, a major figure within mainstream education, the President of the National Union of Teachers, Hilary Bills, argues that 'I don't believe it is a coincidence that the level of disruption in schools has risen at the same time as the curriculum has been narrowed and testing has increased' (Eason, 2005). Steiner held a similar view: 'It is always a matter of concern when someone has passed examinations; he can still undoubtedly be an extremely clever person, but this must be *in spite of* having passed examinations.'

An Education for the Evolution of Consciousness?

'The only way out of this social chaos is to bring spirituality into the souls of people through education, so that out of the spirit itself, people may find the way to progress and the further evolution of civilisation.'

Rudolf Steiner

An education system will tend tacitly to reproduce and reinforce the prevailing values of the society of which it is a part. At the beginning of the 21st century, the dominant world-view is overwhelmingly that of materialism and consumerism – values which increasingly saturate and define mainstream schooling systems and culture more generally (e.g. Schor, 2005). Within education, we are witnessing the uncritical ascendancy of a soulless utilitarianism, in which quantity prevails over quality, academic over artistic and craft-oriented pursuits, ends over means, goals and targets over process – in short, head over heart.

Under such a system, children are being conditioned into the very kind of limited, materialistic consciousness which it is surely humankind's urgent evolutionary imperative to transcend. A cocktail of one-sided materialism and subservience to soulless technology (House, 2004b), allied with an associated chronic loss of meaning, arguably lies at the heart of our emotional and ecological malaise. And an educational approach which merely mimics these same values is bound to reinforce that malaise.

I believe that our education system – in both its overriding philosophy and in its detailed procedures – should be at the forefront of the *evolution of human consciousness* that a spiritually mature way of living and being entails. Steiner (Waldorf) education is positioned right at the forefront of this global wave of educational models which are striving to find a better way to educate our children. In Steiner education our vision is lifted above the materialistic, deterministic world-view of 'modernity', with a concerted attempt being made to understand materialism in its wider evolutionary and cosmic context.

In the preface to his *Mystics after Modernism*, (2000; orig. 1901) Steiner wrote: 'Only those who understand spirit in the sense of *true* mysticism can fully understand the reality of nature.' For Steiner, 'the divine is not something external to be recapitulated as an image in the human spirit. Rather, ...the divine is *awakened* within the human being' – and for Steiner, such awakening must always be an act of freedom for every individual, free of religious dogma of any kind.

At its best, Steiner education maximises the possibility of such a natural, unforced divine awakening – and of a deep-ecological awareness and re-enchantment - through creating a learning environment that continually strives for a balanced engagement of mind, body, soul - and heart. Steiner himself passionately emphasised the urgent need to 'put *the heart* back into education'.

In his book *The Child's Changing Consciousness and Waldorf Education*, Steiner (1988) was a trenchant critic of modernity and its accompanying world-view. While always being careful to acknowledge the positive achievements of modern science, he points out just how much its one-sidedness has 'alienated the human being from himself'. On materialism, his critique is devastating: 'Materialistic minds can grasp only human thinking – and this is their tragedy... Materialism is the one view of the world which has no understanding of what matter is'!... Steiner emphasises how, in the dominant over-intellectualised climate of modern education, there has been a fundamental misunderstanding of children and child development, for 'the child's soul is so entirely different from that of a thoroughly intellectualised grown-up... A pedagogy which only observes outer phenomena does not penetrate into those regions of the human being that reveal what should be done with regard to practical life.'

Steiner championed a truly *living pedagogy* – for 'life is full of living movement, of transformation... it has to be comprehended in all its mobility... and 'partaking in *the creativity of the world* is the very thing our present culture is waiting for'. As Rudolf Meyer puts it, 'The whole of nature is permeated with creative intelligence' (Meyer, 1995). It is hardly surprising, then, that for Steiner, 'If you [the teacher] come with something dead, you inflict wounds upon what is... alive in the child, you attack its sense of truth and reality'.

For Steiner, the antidote to these pernicious forces consists in the qualities of *heart* and *love*. Thus he wrote, 'In our work we need *forces of the heart*... that we ourselves have our heart in our pedagogy' - which is just one reason why he was so opposed to the kind of centrally imposed and determined 'national curriculum' which has now become the norm in mainstream Western education. Steiner maintained that it is teachers who stand in the forefront of bringing new impulses into our civilisation; 'and an awareness has to emerge of how much needs to be changed... before a truly human form of education becomes established'.

The technocratic mentality of 'modernity' and its accompanying myth of materialism – together with their psychological manifestation, self-centred ego-consciousness - are deeply pervasive in modern culture. However, in Steiner education we are quite self-consciously pursuing an education which strives to enable the mature evolution of human consciousness far beyond the one-sided materialism of the prevailing *Zeitgeist*.

Part of this striving entails grappling with the deepest paradoxes of human existence. The Steiner Kindergarten, for example, is *simultaneously* a site of both complexity *and* simplicity: *complexity* in the sense of engaging with the delicate subtleties of soul experience and their experiential dynamics (what Professor Max van Manen calls the 'tone and tact of teaching' - House, 2003); and *simplicity* in the sense that we seek to protect the child from sensory and 'soul' overload in these years, as his/her energies are used to develop the physical body and the nascent imagination. We believe that it is the simple virtues and sensibilities that make us most fully human. To create an environment in which young children have a deep experience of such values and ways-of-being is therefore a core aspiration of our early education.

Child education must surely play a central role in transcending the one-sided world-view of modernity. The environment and the soul-nourishment provided in Steiner education offer one of the greatest hopes for the evolutionary health of humankind, through the expanded, ego-transcending consciousness that we cultivate and model in our Kindergarten environment.

Imagine what the effect might be within just one generation, if all young children were to receive a consistent Steiner (Waldorf) experience in early childhood. Not least, OFSTED's profound concerns about the mounting malaise of early childhood would begin to be addressed seriously and effectively. The Chief Inspector of Schools, David Bell, says that many young children are providing an 'almost intractable' challenge to schools and teachers, with many youngsters 'appearing less prepared for school than they have ever been before', and with 'children never having sat at a table because their parents let them eat sitting on the floor in front of the television' (Begley, 2003).

In Steiner (Waldorf) terms, it is the over-intellectualised culture of modernity which is perhaps chiefly responsible for these maladies – as Rudolf Meyer (1995) puts it: 'mankind's powers of reason [will] not alone be able to find contact again with the creative spirit. What [is] needed is child-like qualities to rejuvenate and permeate our whole being' (the last century's greatest scientist, Albert Einstein, did not learn to read and write until into his early teens, and spent much of his early childhood in the kind of unawakened, unintruded-upon 'dream-consciousness' which we actively cultivate in the Steiner Kindergarten.)

In summary, then, in Steiner education we find a fully articulated approach to re-balancing the potentially catastrophic one-sidedness of modern materialistic culture.

Conclusion

'Slow schools give scope for invention and response to cultural change, while fast schools just turn out the same old burgers.'

Professor Maurice Holt

'Education... can now move from competition-driven modes of operation to conducting daily affairs as if every other person truly mattered. Children can now be instilled with delight in life, not just the conquest of winning.'

Robert Sardello, Ph.D.

Recent research findings in a wide diversity of fields are amply confirming the educational approach devised by Rudolf Steiner almost a century ago. Schools and teachers across the globe will testify to the fact that Rudolf Steiner has bequeathed the most comprehensive holistic framework for education that has ever been articulated.

As modern mainstream education systems lurch from inevitable crisis to crisis, the education world could do no better than to pay close attention to, and learn from, the Steiner pedagogical approach to child development and learning, which is successfully facilitating the development of many thousands of responsible, creative, well-rounded and emotionally intelligent young people the world over.

'For real life, love is the greatest power of knowledge. And without this love it is utterly impossible to attain to a knowledge of man which could form the basis of a true art of education.'
'There are three effective methods of education – fear, ambition and love. We will do without the first two.'
'Receive the children with reverence; educate them with love; relinquish them in freedom.'

Rudolf Steiner

Richard House graduated from Oxford University with first class honours (Geography) in 1976. With a Ph.D. in Environmental Sciences (UEA), he is a trained Steiner (Waldorf) class and Kindergarten teacher, a founder-member of the Norfolk Initiative Steiner School, Series Editor of the acclaimed Hawthorn Press 'Early Years' series, and a professional counsellor and psychotherapist. He writes regularly on educational and psychotherapeutic issues for various professional journals and magazines, with over 250 publications to his name to date. His book Therapy Beyond Modernity was published in 2003 (Karnac Books), and his forthcoming books With an Independent Voice: Critical Essays on Therapy and Counselling and The Trouble with Education will be published in 2006 by PCCS Books and Ur Publications respectively. Correspondence: richardahouse@hotmail.com

References

A comprehensive list of references, including selected writings of Rudolf Steiner, is available on www.excite-education.org

EMBODYING[1] CREATIVITY

Ruth Nolan

Imagining a Future Classroom

As I walk into the classroom, the first thing I notice is the absence of solid walls. I seem to have entered an outdoor domed enclosure; comfortable, shaded, sheltered, full of natural light, filtered by moving, green leaves. The air smells fresh and is moving gently and quietly, hardly enough to stir the plants arranged around the perimeter of the room. I can also hear water trickling. Students of mixed ages and genders are seated on small cushions on the polished, warm floor, fanning out in semicircles around a makeshift stage area containing a set made of roughly improvised draped cloth and a few dramatically placed found objects. Mozart's Requiem fills the air, as if the orchestra and choir are present in the room.

All attention is riveted on the two players, centre stage, who are miming with great drama, a scene they have improvised, representing a moment in history, from the Second World War. Three more players wind their way through the audience to join the action on stage and the play reaches its climax and ends, leaving the audience in the grip of the horror portrayed on stage. The adult mentor stands and instructs the audience to rise and, with movement, represent how they feel about what they have just seen. There is silence broken only by the sounds of bare feet slapping the floor, as the audience writhes

---

[1] Realising that 'embodied' might not yet be everyday language, and is also one word describing a multiplicity of experiencing, some explanation follows: For an instant experience of being embodied, take off your shoes and socks and walk across the room, having first dropped a box of drawing pins on the floor. The way you are, as you tread carefully, all ears, eyes and present to the tips of your toes, is embodied. To stay that way for any length of time, without the prod of danger or discomfort, takes practice, if you are over five, own a pair of shoes and live in a Western country. Sportsmen, musicians, actors, artists, dancers and criminals all need to be good at this in order to prosper in their chosen field.
Further information about embodiment may be found at www.excite-education.org

representing the horror and agony they understand to be an experience of war. "And now, with sound!" Immediately the air is filled with the audience's sounds of screaming, sirens wailing, machine gun fire, shouting, sobbing and weeping.

A gong sounds, silence falls over the room and the audience and players are guided to sit in stillness, and then, as they feel ready, to move to the perimeter of the room and collect paper and pastels, to return to their cushions and represent their experience in colour and shape. The mentor instructs the students to give their representations a title and then the drawings are collected by the players, taken to a veranda area, blue tacked onto screens and sprayed with fixative. While this is happening, the mentor is leading the class through a series of stretches and visualisations, designed not only to relieve any tension in the body, but also to maintain the connection between the mind and the body. Breath and movement restores connection with the earth, balances both sides of the brain and relaxes the students into an alert engagement with the next improvised, short performance.

These short, hastily improvised plays and sets have been put together by the small groups of players working together after sharing discoveries made through their private research, via internet, library and text books. Their grouping has come about through self-selecting around topics raised by the whole group, after listening to a story read by the mentor, in an earlier class. After reviewing the response of the audience, each student writes notes in key word format and quick visual representing, and returns to become the audience for the next play. There are twenty-five students in this group, and each play lasts for 5 minutes, with 10 minutes of response and preparation time between plays. After an hour and fifteen minutes, the mentor hands round the notes prepared by each group and then gives the instructions for homework. "Selecting any of the five topics you have witnessed, or participated in today, write about what you now know about fascism and war, that is new to you, using further research to investigate your area of interest. You can choose your mode of writing from the following: newspaper report, main story TV news item, screenplay, documentary, essay, or poem. Hand your research notes in with your final work. Remember to document your sources. Ask for help from the IT and library staff - they are there to assist your research. At our next meeting, we will discuss issues arising out of your research and your experiences today."

"Thank you for your splendid participation in today's class. I felt moved by the sincerity of your work today. If you feel inspired to work any of these cameos up for our end of term performance on the main stage, better book a place now - space is filling up fast. Collect your visual representings and add them to your portfolios, to be used for inspiration when you are writing, and to be kept for our final day of clustering for this subject."

As the students leave the classroom, and pull on their shoes, I notice that some of them look pensive and thoughtful, others, relieved to be moving out of the heaviness of war and others hurrying to let off steam outdoors. There are a few Monty Python clowns, goose stepping in unison, with one arm raised and the other held under their noses, representing Hitler's moustache.

What I noticed most about my experience of the class was that every student was fully engaged.

This reminds me of when I was at primary school, in the palm of my teacher's hand, along with the rest of the class, being read a story. The teacher's voice rose and fell and her lips curled in disdain, her eyebrows arched with surprise, and always her eyes moving from the text to her audience, holding us in her spell. We were engaged in relationship with her, hanging on every word, present to every nuance. It was a warm spring afternoon and I can still remember her name - Miss Brooker - the smell of the breeze, the blackbird's song in the background, and a bluebottle buzzing lazily.

Retaining the Magic of Education

There is no reason for the magic of education to be left behind with childhood. We only have to return to our senses, and I mean that quite literally, to recapture the rapture we felt as children.

I teach Creative Process to a small group of adult artists, and a large group of adults who sing together, but probably do not consider themselves to be singers. At the beginning of every class, we take the time to get ourselves warmed up and "embodied'. This takes 30 minutes in the two-hour singing class, and is partly necessary to prevent damage to the vocal chords because we sing in a full bodied, boisterous way.

If we are not using much sound in the creative process class, embodying and imaginative warm ups are typically shorter. I may teach a Samoan clap dance for example, which makes my students laugh because, they say, it is entirely impossible to think whilst clapping the complicated patterns. With such busy minds that are usually multi-tracking, my students say that it is refreshing to have a rest from the frantic noise of their minds, and very pleasurable. As they sink deeper into their bodies, they find unexpected emotions arising; unacknowledged grief, tears, joy and laughter, and a well of knowledge and inspiration they did not know they had. All very useful for artistic expression or singing, I hear you say, but how might this be relevant for maths and literacy?

One of my students, Georgie Munro, is a volunteer at her children's secondary school, working with students experiencing difficulty with some aspect of their literacy. She was asked to work on the literacy skills of 13-15 year old boys, who had failed the existing teaching system for reading and stuttered their way painfully through simple texts. Georgie noticed, after some weeks of observation, that the students had picked up most of the basic skills required for successful reading, yet made frequent mistakes. Guessing that the students might have a fear of reading aloud and might have felt humiliated by making mistakes in the past, Georgie experimented with some ideas to remove fear, adapted from exercises used in my Creative Process class.

After the exercises, Georgie had each student read a couple of pages, with remarkable results. The students had gone from making at least one mistake in approximately every two lines, to reading a whole page without a mistake. Stuttering and stumbling was replaced with confidence and fluidity. Georgie then had the students create a positive statement about reading, using key words generated by the exercises.

The sentences produced by the four students, exactly reproduced, were:

* "I think I read better. I feel confident now I can do it. Now I reckon I will read for the rest of my life."

* "I am now more confident and a faster reader, I am finding it easier to read."

* "Reading is a big success for me. Its fun, enjoyment and I am calm about it."

* "Getting better for sure. Today I paused only once. It's beginning to become fun, reading aloud. Handwriting and spelling getting the hang of."

The impact lasted and was improved on during the next six months. Georgie has written instructions for the steps she followed, in full, for anyone who would like to try this experiment. *(See the SEI website,* www.excite-education.org *)*

Making use of the so-called 'right side of the brain' for creative problem solving and innovation as well as art, has been well championed by writers like Vincent Nolan, Betty Edwards and Edward de Bono. 'Emotional Intelligence' has been championed by Daniel Goleman and writers like the depth psychologists: Thomas Moore, James Hillman and Robert Sardello, who also dare to speak of 'heart' and 'soul'. For me the most exciting direction is that of the phenomenologists, such as David Abram, whose compelling work, 'The Spell of the Sensuous' champions the sensing body as the vehicle for receiving, storing and re-accessing knowledge. It is our bodies that receive all stimuli, and our brains are the body organs that process our bodies' sensing. Our bodies store so much information, and through our bodies and movement, we can become aware of much that we have forgotten.

When the mind is focussed within the body and in the present moment, a paradigm shift is allowed to occur. Suddenly, I am no longer a separate being standing outside existence and looking in as an observer. Now I am part of existence, pulsing in relationship to every single thing around me. The line between animate and inanimate becomes less well defined, as rocks and teacups become enlivened with this new consciousness. The world throbs and pulsates, and things lose their hard edges, to become more mutable, as in an Impressionist's painting. The line between subject and object, I and it, wobbles and melts away, so that we are now beings in a state of constant flux, as we respond and resonate with each other, defined more by the spaces between us than by an outline that contains us.

This may sound alarming to most of us who grew up in the positivist paradigm, where facts are hard facts, unchanging and provable, and we can feel safe in some provable certainties. There is solid ground under our feet and the superiority of knowing that I am the subject and everything else is an object, and I can separate my mind from my body and my experience, and so be objective about the nature of reality. The paradigm shift that has occurred in Science and Maths, due to quantum physics, has not really trickled into the consciousness of the population at large. Whereas the physicists speak in terms of matter being made up of strings and membranes existing in eleven dimensions, so that a table is now more a symphony in wood than a bunch of molecules and atoms, most of us are still thinking in black and white, and the table is inanimate and unchanging. We are still the products of our positivist education, with ideas of right and wrong and debating, a paradigm that is still upheld by our legal and political systems.

Our fascination for Eastern mysticism and our curiosity and romanticism about the ancient tribal ways of Native Americans, Indigenous Australians and our Celtic ancestors, perhaps stem from an instinctive understanding that something was lost when we moved into the positivist paradigm, and we may need to look to our human roots to rediscover what that was.

David Abram traces the beginning of this shift to the development of alphabetic written language, as it became available to people at large, outside the priesthood. In cultures where stories are still told, or sung, rather than written, the split of mind and body, subject and object, does not seem to have occurred. The way that these indigenous cultures speak of their world seems childish, primitive and superstitious to the uninitiated, but, suddenly, it all makes sense when we apply phenomenological disciplines of suspending that which we think we know and instead allowing an embodied experience of what is. Perhaps we will discover after all that there really are fairies at the bottom of the garden.

As we have developed our cognitive minds and our ability to disconnect from our bodies and all that surrounds us, we seem to have lost our capacity for awe and wonder. We have lost trust in our intuition, instinct and wisdom, and rely instead on external authority, experts and machines. For magic, spirituality, ecstasy and expansive connection, we are now dependent on drugs, or fundamentalism.

There is no need to wait for the future to arrive. Methods of reconnecting and maintaining embodied presence in the classroom are being practised already in Australia, pioneered by MIECAT, the Melbourne Institute of Experiential Creative and Art Therapy, where theory is translated into experiential practice in the methods used to train therapists. Embodied methods have long been the basis of dance and drama classes around the world, and are central to martial arts, yoga and meditation. Perhaps shamanism and the ancient art of story telling, with song and dance, can teach us something about education too. It is a question of integrating existing creative and embodied practice into the school classroom.

Subjects need not be disconnected from each other. Let's see Art, Maths and Music taught in the same classroom, they are, after all, intimately connected. Surely biology, geology and anthropology would make geography lessons much more interesting, and why not combine them with history and archaeology? Why must our students choose between philosophy, music, literature and art? They are all interconnected, why not teach them that way?

I agree with John Ralston Saul, who suggests we need a creative workforce to meet the rapid change we confront, and I suggest therefore that we need creativity to be modelled by embodied, creative teachers. Let's have some "effervescent imaginative disorder" in our schools. Surely engaged fascinated students would reduce the need for the regimentation that schools of the past have employed to keep order.

The English education system was based on a military model; a model designed to prevent people thinking for themselves. If we want a mature population that can think for itself, we must begin by giving our teachers creative and embodying tools and the time and space to apply them. There is no need to teach children how to think creatively; they could do that very well before they went to school. What's needed is the understanding provided by creative pioneers of how to remove the barriers to creativity and learning that education normally instils. Collaborative structures that develop innovation, such as the Synectics Process and the MIECAT Process, can be applied to manage the integration of the cognitive, with imagination, movement, emotion and creative expression. All those students who are currently having their imaginative, collaborative, emotional and creative capabilities knocked out of them at school, would benefit.

Scientists and teachers are showing interest in how to measure creativity. My personal measure is to register the amount of smiling, laughter, engagement, concentration and the speed of learning. For example, if I play with some improvised, collaborative, rhythm work before teaching a new song, I notice that my singers learn the new song quickly and with less than usual effort, on my part and theirs. Also, the harmonies are likely to be more exact and the whole group experiences a sense of satisfaction and pleasure, measured by smiles, laugher and a relaxed, focussed stillness.

This kind of creativity measuring also works in more serious groups. For example, in the last facilitator training I conducted, the laughter was so raucous and prolonged that people were drawn from all over the building to see what they were missing out on. The training was for the peer facilitators of Family Support Groups; people who care for someone with an alcohol or other drug problems. These were people who were confronting every day, the pain, fear and despair of their children being heroin addicts. The laughter came about through an unplanned series of improvised role-plays, which were used to test theories arising from the group, about how to deal with difficult group members. On this occasion, I had completely departed from my running sheet and allowed the group to collaborate on some problem solving.

No-one was upset by the unexpected change in direction from the programme, and I believe more was learnt, because I was able to have the flexibility to follow the needs arising from the group, rather than imposing my own theory of what they needed to know. If teachers in schools could be allowed to have the same flexibility, I believe they would have a better rate of engagement with their students, more success with creating the climate for learning, less time lost to discipline problems and less time lost to sickness and truancy.

According to John Cleese (1994), humour is also a useful creativity tool in itself:
"Ordinary, common-or-garden laughter is the easiest way for us to get into the open mode" It is easy to move from open, creative mode to closed, logical mode when the need for focussed action demands it, and once there, to get stuck in a groove. Humour and laughter move us back into creative and therefore open-minded mode, which is the place we need to be for learning. And best of all, laughter is a pleasurable, embodying experience.

"I set no theory upon you
but try to resonate to the deeper truth"

Ruth Nolan was informally trained in the Synectics process from the age of fourteen, as her parents practised their pioneering skills at home. She has experimented with creative process techniques in all areas of her life - parenting, teaching, counselling, problem solving, community development, music and artwork. Her formal training was in Art and Design at West Surrey College of Art and Design, UK, with postgraduate studies in Creative Arts Therapy at MIECAT, Australia. Work experience includes teaching pottery at TAFE to Indigenous Australian adults, teaching pottery to children in schools, conducting training for facilitators, training alcohol and other drug counsellors, teaching singing to adults, counselling, conducting, and musical directing for community choirs.

Reference

Abram, D. (1997) *The Spell of the Sensuous.* New York: Vintage Books.
Edwards, B. (1982) *Drawing on the Right Side of the Brain.* Great Britain: Fontana/Collins.
Goleman, D. (1996) *Emotional Intelligence.* London: Bloomsbury Publishing.
Hillman, J. (1997) *The Soul's Code: In Search of Character and Calling* USA: Warner Books.
Moore, T. (1994) *Care of the Soul* USA: Perennial
Nawal El Saadawi (2002) ABC Fine Music Radio Interview with Margaret Throsby. 3/6/02
Nolan, V. (1991) *The Innovator's Handbook.* London: Sphere Books Ltd.
Parbury, S. (2004) MIECAT Graduation Haiku.
Ralston Saul, J. (1999) *Citizenship vs The Reigning Linear Trap.* Public Lecture at University of South Australia, 29/8/99: ABC.
Sardello, R. (1996) *Love and the Soul.* USA: Perennial.
Skynner, R. & Cleese, J. (1994) *Life and how to survive it.* London: Mandarin Paperbacks.

CAN SCHOOLS BE REPLACED?

Cedric Cullingford

Pupils' views of schools

Schools are based on an outdated model, suitable perhaps for the factory age but no longer appropriate. This much might be easily acknowledged, but the sad fact is that schools have been wrong from the start. The perception that schools do not work is a result of the growing gap between the political view of the education system, with the central control of the National Curriculum, the management of teachers through literacy and numeracy hours supported by inspection, and the unease of those who see a disenchanted, apathetic and unhappy society lacking the skills of creativity and entrepreneurship that the policy is supposed to promote. The manifestations of control are ever more astringent, internationally, with ever more targets, league tables, naming and shaming, all the rhetoric of those who see the policy, as one exasperated commentator put it, as "doomed to success", since targets, however meaningless, will always be met, and every policy, however incoherent, will be a sign of a politician's strenuous activity.

This chapter, however, is based on the experience of pupils who are in schools, and on extensive research, exploring what schools are like for them and ascertaining what pupils would find both ideal and more appropriate (1). The fundamental conclusion is that schools are a disastrous mistake. It is not that they are out of date but wrong from the start. Pupils have always suffered from tests, competition, bullying, humiliation, unfairness and have always been presented with an impression of society as mean, unforgiving, hierarchical and indifferent to their opinions. Some would say that schools need to teach children the brutalities of society, to toughen them up. Pupils would not agree, since this is a self-fulfilling prophecy justified by those who have emerged from the rite of passage, not those immersed in it.

What would education be like if we listened to (and heard) those in it? Education would be based on what we know of human development, especially in the early years, through all the research on cognition, on emotional development and intelligence and behaviour. (2) Education would not be based on the imposition of a set curriculum packed with what seems like arbitrary facts and antipathetic to individual critical thinking.

The first three years are crucial, since character and conduct depend on what happens then. We know how crucial these years are, yet we largely ignore them. Young children, with their intelligent gaze, their need for relationships, their ontological neutrality and their personal traumas, need all the help they can get. So do their parents, since parenting is the most difficult of all human skills.

Young children use their critical gaze not only to categorise and make sense of the physical world but to look closely at people, their points of view, the distinctions between truth and falsehood and others' emotional needs. Young children need strong, intellectual relationships with adults from the beginning. Parenting classes would not be a stigma for those deemed to be failing, but would involve the whole community, grandparents and the retired being a rich source, but with as many adults as possible involved. The intellectual relationship that children yearn for is the sharing of curiosity, of concepts and stories, of an exploration of the world, aural and visual, emotional and perceptive. The fundamental question that young children want answering is 'why are we as we are?' just as they later ask 'why do people in institutional roles behave so differently?'

The innate intellectual curiosity is a need, not a luxury. Young children ask fundamental questions about God, the nature of the Universe and about society. Some cynics suggest that since these are such difficult questions to answer we send them to school where they are taught not to question at all.

The curiosity of young children needs to be stimulated as much as possible, rather than suppressed; the sharing of stories, sounds and sights is crucial. Young children are constantly receiving information about the world, the divides between the rich and poor, questions of justice and injustice, and they need support in making sense of this. At the moment information about the real world is officially ignored at school.

Pupils and Teachers

The provision of secure relationships would not altogether protect children from trauma - these can come from overheard remarks and misinterpretations - but they would give young children confidence, motivation and the fundamental sense that they are sharing understanding and that this is pleasurable. Children love to learn, but they resent being taught.

This is a fundamental dilemma for teachers. From pupils' point of view, teachers are there to impose a given set of facts. The pupils' task is not to think but to guess what it is that the teacher wants them to say. All questions are closed, so that the intelligence of pupils is diverted from thinking into working out what is required, a task at which it is very easy to fail.

Pupils, throughout their schooling, long for individual relationships with adults. They regret the fact that there are such few opportunities to talk as an individual with teachers. Teachers are far too busy. Even opportunities like field trips are now rare because of the culture of fear and risk. Pupils do not want teachers just to impose discipline, to sustain their role. They want teachers also to be people. In fact, they want to learn from adults with their private enthusiasms, not from teachers. In the circumstances of school there are few opportunities for teachers to be human.

In all the articles about 'my favourite teacher' one fact stands out and that is not the prowess of the teacher but the personal connection and interest. Just think for a moment of an outstanding lesson at school and it is bound to be outside the normal curriculum, something different, something that engaged the teacher's personal interest.

For pupils, schools and teachers (however brilliant their endeavours) are a fundamental problem. Fortunately, the natural human curiosity is such that the problem can by bypassed. In the first three years we note that the curiosity of children is directed in certain ways. They ask why things are as they are and not just what. They are curious not just about the physical world but the social one. They want to know about people and relationships and the way people organise themselves. They have experience of small groups, at home, and need far more than this, because it gives them the opportunity to share and explore ideas.

This drive for understanding, this fundamental need to comprehend the nature of the world they find themselves in would lead to a fundamentally different curriculum. Instead of the tokenism of 'citizenship', the moral questions of society would be central. It would also be exciting since it is these questions that are at the heart of all art, music and literature, as well as the curiosity that drives science.

If young children are influenced in particular by those who do not have designs on them and are interested in the topics that attract adults, then their early experiences would be quite different. Firstly they would not be deprived of information, like pictures and music, but would be steeped in visual and aural awareness.

The ideal space

Let us take as example a subject that few would associate with children: architecture. All the evidence demonstrates that children are very sensitive to space and to aesthetics. Space is not just a psychological concept but a manifestation of children's awareness of the environment. Schools are ugly places, not just in terms of the litter but in the paucity of proper provision and sense of occasion. Children are not interested in wall displays compared to real pictures of the kind that adults like. Children react against the visual illiteracy of inner cities, the aesthetic degradation.

The ideal spaces for children to learn are those places that are rich in stimulation. In place of schools they would want museums, art-galleries and libraries, just those places sought out by educated adults. It is there that they would have the opportunity to talk to others, to find out what interests people and the sources of information.

Pupils want to look for, and find, answers to their questions rather than having answers imposed on them. In all the many experiments on successful pupils, the findings are always the same; the desire and opportunity to learn, to question and to think, is far more efficacious than the imposition of facts to be tested. Letting pupils learn rather than teaching them raises standards, but makes teachers and administrators uncomfortable.

If the fundamental question children ask is why the world is like this, then there are a number of routes that can assuage their curiosity. One lies in scientific experiment. The physical world is fascinating in itself, from the fundamentals of structure and mechanics to mathematical models. Young children's attempts to explain scientific facts are more interesting (and instructive) than a rigid answer that bores them. The concept of 'play' is driven by the urge to explore the physical world.

Very soon the curiosity about the environment is joined by the need to explore the great dilemmas, the controversial issues, like global climate change and pollution. This moral curiosity also drives the need to understand history, not the history of dates from 1066 and all that but looking back at explanations of why we live in the world as it now is. The inheritance and the personal experience of individuals - real people again - is what interests children.

Young children often seek the answers to their questions in any other source than school, from their peers, from parents, from the media like television and from the Internet. Their prowess with information and communication systems is well known and contrasts with their boredom with school. When there are so many alternative sources of information, school is reduced to a kind of social centre, a place for handing in assignments.

The basic principles of the future education system will apply to all ages. There will not be ambivalent concepts like 'nurseries', 'life-long learning', 'key stages' and the 'core curriculum'. There needs to be a purpose that engages all learning, rather than the refusal even to think about its purpose. At the present time, when pupils from infant schools upwards are asked about the purpose of schooling, they say it is to help them get jobs. We need to put the emphasis on the excitement of education and understanding as itself the fundamental purpose of life.

The ideal curriculum

The basic principles will put the emphasis on education from birth. There will be many locations, of the kind that are attractive to be in. These can include community centres, but they would be aesthetically appealing, as unlike schools and prisons as possible.

Everyone would be involved in education, in satisfying the need for young people to talk, to enquire and to be helped in understanding. We do not always know the answers, but we have never met anyone who did not have pleasure in being asked. Sharing enthusiasms and interests is not a chore. Dialogue, discussions and information would be open-ended.

Children would be encouraged to specialise in particular interests, like music, or whatever attracts them, since they would be aware of all the other possibilities and alternative ways of answering the fundamental questions. There would be no need to 'cover 'the curriculum, but emphasis placed on critical thinking, on philosophical dialogue. Stories of all kinds would be the means of understanding human behaviour.

As much support as possible would be given to the home, the home as a source of knowledge and not confined to parents. Instead of the fashion of blaming parents, they should be supported. Instead of providing day care so that parents can earn money to satisfy the Treasury, the huge value of good parenting should be recognised. Such a policy would, of course, save billions of pounds in the subsequent costs of crime, ignorance and anti-social behaviour.

The support for the home should include helping to make it as richly resourced an environment as possible. Poverty, and all it symbolises, should no longer be so blandly accepted, even if only for the sake of education.

All young children need to be given the opportunity to talk about matters of interest to them so that we would not have such a high prevalence of autism in society, of individuals barely able to function in a range of literacies.

All these modest suggestions could be backed by evidence that would make the references longer than the chapter itself; all are based on the experience of young children. The purpose of education, the nature of the curriculum and the state of institutions would be fundamentally different.

All this would raise standards considerably whilst saving copious amounts of money. So why is nothing done about it? Most of us are deeply and unknowingly affected by the education system. To suggest that it is fundamentally flawed and that it causes much trauma is widely recognised and rarely denied, even by those in it. And yet, the system implacably continues. There are ingrained habits as well as vested interests. There are the assumptions that what was bad enough for us is good enough for others and should be inflicted on them. There is the desire to control, to dictate policy, to show who is boss, whatever the consequences. It is rather like that anecdote of the nun going to the mother superior and saying 'But it's not true, is it' and receiving the reply 'No, dear, its not but don't tell the others'.

The fundamental problem with a system 'doomed to success' is that as we recognise it failing there are ever more strenuous attempts to force it in the same direction. It is like the failure of torture in the Inquisition; the answer was to try even harder.

We do not always recognise how bad things are in schools. This is partly because of the resilience of human beings who survive the most difficult of circumstances. It is partly because of the efforts of teachers who do their heroic best despite the system. It is partly because the world of politics and the media are a world of their own, cut off from everyday reality. And it is partly because parents have been cajoled into thinking only of their own offspring and that the present system is the only way to do so. Most of all, this indifference to what is happening, and has been happening for 150 years, is because to acknowledge that something is wrong would be to have to accept some responsibility in putting it right and that for most is a step too far.

One day there will be an education system based on the principles described, but that will be the day when people accept the evidence about the intelligence and trauma of young children. Meanwhile things will stumble on and the conflicts and unhappiness continue, and all the excuses of blame, from religion to 'that is the nature of things' will prevail, rather than the responsibilities of cure.

The only alternative to all this hopeless activity - "The best lack all conviction; the worst are full of passionate intensity"- is a growing, collective realisation of the truth. We see many signs of teachers themselves understanding this, when they have time to think. We know the disquiet of parents. But there is still passivity in the face of what appear to be implacable institutions. It is when they are exposed in all their inner contradictions that the great change will occur. The first change is acknowledging the facts. Young people know what it is like. How long can their witness be suppressed?

Perhaps the way to kick-start the change can be found first in contemplating a simple proposal: abolish schools. It is not unthinkable - in fact Ivan Illich (3) proposed it in 1976 - but it is not considered. It would certainly force a rethink; it would be like taking into account the equally convincing fact that, despite the famous assertion, prison does not work. It might not be possible instantly to abolish prisons (or schools) but taking the possibility seriously might make alternatives more feasible. Meanwhile we could create a complete programme for all children from birth to three. Despite the well-meaning rhetoric behind Surestart, one of the recent initiatives, this is a programme both too institutional and too late. A real intervention at the start - that would make a difference and force a re-think of the rest of the system.

Biographical Note

Professor Cedric Cullingford is at the University of Huddersfield. Recent books include *'The Human Experience; the Early Years'* *'Prejudice'* ' The Causes of *Exclusion* ' and *'The Best Years of their Lives? Pupils' experience of school'*

Reference

(1) e.g. Cedric Cullingford *"The Best Years of their lives? Pupils' experience of school"* London, Kogan Page 2001. *"The Human Experience; the Early Years"* Aldershot, Ashgate 1999.
(2) E.g. Demasio, A *The Feeling of what happens; Body, Emotion and the making of consciousness.* London, Heineman 2001. Pinker, S *The Blank State; the Modern Denial of Human Nature,* London Allen Lane 2002
(3) Ivan Illich *"Deschooling Society"* Harmondsworth, Penguin Books, 1976

The books of Matt Ridley are a popular summary of some of the issues.

THINKING, LEARNING, AND CREATIVITY

George M. Prince
With Victoria Logan (teacher)

Introduction

Designing any process requires that we understand what the process is intended to accomplish. From the dictionary, we obtain: "Education: a knowledge or skill obtained or developed by a learning process". So, the learning process is fundamental to education.

Dictionary definitions of learning focus on *objectives* but do not tell us much about the *process* of learning. Underlying learning is the process of *thinking*. We go through the process of thinking to *create* meaning. We create meaning by making a connection between the new information and what we already know, so that the new information 'makes sense'. This is not necessarily instantaneous; we may require several iterations, in a process of trial and error. And in particular instances, we may never 'get it' – there is no guarantee that the process will succeed

This description of the process of 'thinking to learn' sounds surprisingly like that of 'creative thinking' to produce new ideas, concepts, products, etc. New ideas are the result of making connections between material that has not previously been connected – what Koestler called *bisociation* (1). This too will probably require a number of iterations and may not succeed. Learning and creativity are both, basically, the ability to make connections to create meaning or significance.

Consider all thinking as on a spectrum. At one end is the kind of thinking where you connect with things you have already learned - like a policeman making a stop signal. At the other end of the spectrum is a puzzle or problem and you need an idea to solve the problem. But you do not have any connection making material to put together with your information to create an idea.

The ability (and willingness) to pull some connection making possibilities out of that situation and create an idea no one has ever had before, is the most difficult kind of creative thinking. Here is an example:

Alastair Pilkington was in charge of making plate glass in a plant in England. The process consisted of pouring molten glass on a polished sheet of steel, letting it cool, and then turning it over and polishing out the imperfections made by the steel. It was, Pilkington thought, a clumsy process but he had been unable to think of a way to improve it. No matter how he polished the surface of that steel, it still left impressions in the glass.

One night as Pilkington was washing the dishes, he noticed a patch of grease floating on the surface. Grease has nothing to do with glass, but Pilkington was a connection-maker, and he pursued his observation. He was transfixed. The under-side of that grease was perfectly smooth because the water was smooth!

He had it! Float the plate glass on water and it would be perfect! One trouble, he immediately thought: when the hot molten glass hit the water, the water would explode into steam..... Not good! But again, he did not give up. The idea was sound, just find a liquid that would not explode in the heat.

After many experiments, Pilkington perfected Float Glass. He floated the molten glass on molten tin and produced perfect plate glass every time. It revolutionised the industry.

Going back to the spectrum of thinking, at one end, as we said, there is the connecting with information I already have, like the policeman. At the other end is the kind of thinking that Pilkington did (forcing a connection with a seeming irrelevance) and in the middle of our spectrum or scale are the connections I make when I am creating a learning that is new to *me*, though not to the world

Thinking to learn

An example of that might be my granddaughter Marjorie and the lighthouse. When she was little she came to visit me at a place I had near the ocean. She arrived late in the evening and when she went to her room, there was the flash of a lighthouse that lit up the room. She didn't know about lighthouses and looked startled, so I said, "That flash is the light in the lighthouse. It is to warn ships of danger."

She looked pleased and said, "Oh, it's like the top of a police car." She had made a connection that made sense of the lighthouse experience

So, creative thinking and thinking to learn are very similar – they are both the ability to make connections to make meaning. Everyone can do it because we all need to do it; some people can do it marvellously well. Since all of us have to continually make connections in order to create ideas and understand, it would seem that all of us should be in practice and be such good connection-makers that we could all be terrifically good at learning and creativity. I believe I can suggest a reason why some people are and some are not.

When my son, Winthrop, was a little boy, we were driving along somewhere and he saw his first horse. He grabbed my arm and said excitedly, "Daddy! There is a big cat!" I laughed, and said, "No, Winthrop, that is not a cat, it is a horse."

Actually, what he had done was excellent connection-making to information he had. But I failed to acknowledge that. I just told him his connection-making was wrong.

Doing that to Winthrop once is not critical, but when it happens to him over and over again, at home and at school, those put downs hurt. He begins to feel anxious when asked to make connections. He is afraid he will be wrong and will be disapproved of. He becomes less willing to think and learn.

Contrast that with another true story. My grandson, Max, was visiting me at the place on the ocean. There was one of those big fire extinguishers in the hall beside his bedroom door. He wanted to know what it was, and when he heard, he wanted to squirt it, but I persuaded him not to.

Several weeks later he was visiting the Aquarium, and there was a scuba diver down with the fishes for some reason. Max had never seen a scuba diver, and it captured his full attention. Observing the fire extinguisher tank on the man's back, after a moment he said to his mom, "Mom! There is a fireman!" Beautiful connection–making, and by then Mom knew enough to admire his connection-making before explaining how this tank was different from the fire extinguisher he had seen.

If we are respectful enough of all of a child's trial connection-making, the chances are he will be a daring connection-maker and able to operate at the Pilkington end of the scale. He will also be a very good learner.

Research and Development into Creative Processes

In the early 1960's my company, Synectics Inc., began to offer a creative service. In the interest of learning more about our process we began to audiotape our sessions. In reviewing these tapes, we learned that there was a lot going on that was not visible in the rapid give and take of a session. We later shifted to videotape and discovered even more.

In review, it became our practice to stop the tape whenever *anything* happened. We would then ask "What happened?" When we agreed on what it was, we asked, "Will this increase or decrease the probability of success?" If the answer was "Increase" we asked, "How can we get more of this?" If the answer was "Decrease", we asked, "How do we get less of this?" Because many of the actions that decreased probability also had elements that increased the probability of success, it became clear that the intent was good, but the effect could be damaging.

These videotape studies continued over many years and it allowed us to "see" the negative consequences of many behaviours that had previously seemed acceptable. For example, we had thought it normal and useful for someone to point out a flaw in an idea when they saw it. Experience taught us that this practice killed beginning ideas, which, when pursued, might develop into winners. This led to the practice of withholding negatives until the idea was "built"; only then could it be evaluated, and then only in a friendly and positive way.

When a group learned to operate avoiding the actions that decrease probability of success, they became superior creative problem solvers. In repeated experiments where trained teams competed with teams not trained in the positive practices, the trained teams were far more successful. This suggested that these practices might be usefully applied to any situation where creativity, thinking, *or learning* were important.

In the course of our research into what goes on in invention sessions, it gradually became evident that whenever a person was corrected, contradicted, ignored, or discounted in *any* way, they would 'get even' with the discounter. We could verify this by tracking back from a destructive comment or action to the trigger discount. Questioned, the person discounted would remember their thinking as they "got even", but often not the triggering discount. When it became clear that *everyone* - woman, man, and child - is triggered by a discount and gets revenge in one way or another, we began to wonder: why this hypersensitivity to discounts?

Insights from leading psychologists and psychiatrists like Sullivan, Kegan and Perry provided some explanations. Recent brain research has revealed the mechanism of this reaction.

The origins of Discount/Revenge

The infant and child (and adult) must deal with the genetic imperative: survive! The brain's principal equipment for survival is the amygdala complex. The hypothalamus receives *all* incoming sensations and information. It forwards the information to the appropriate circuits except when there is a hint of threat. If the answer is "yes" or "maybe", the information is sent to the amygdala by express for evaluation.

The amygdala complex begins to play a major role in character formation early in life. About the fifth or sixth month, the infant experiences the threat signal from the amygdala. It is an urgent and powerful signal and is named anxiety.

Long before brain research discovered the mechanism, Harry Stack Sullivan, the great psychiatrist, taught that anxiety is an *uncanny* feeling, akin to awe, dread, loathing, and horror. Unlike hunger or pain, it has no source on which one can focus to alleviate it. Instincts 'believe' that if abandoned, *one will cease to be.* The signals they send are as urgent and compelling as Mother Nature can design. When one senses anxiety, *thinking stops.* The self–system urgently mobilises to initiate immediate action to prevent annihilation. One is dedicated to defence. This direct, solid, instant connection from anxiety to reaction is a significant influence on behaviour all our lives.

The need to be and feel meaningful is not an option. It originates in our genes as a mechanism for survival. "Meaning...is the primary human motion, irreducible..." "Well–fed, warm and free of disease, you may still perish if you cannot "mean." (Kegan, *The Evolving Self)*

The extraordinary impact of any threat to meaningfulness comes from its reverberations with the infant's *genetic apprehension of ceasing to exist* developed in the first year and observed as fear of abandonment. It is this feeling we call *anxiety.*

We never outgrow this need to "mean". To be "seen, to be recognised, however it changes in the complexity of its form, may never change in its intensity.....what an organism does, as William Perry says, is organise; and what a human organism organises is meaning. Thus it is not that a person makes meaning, as much as that *the activity of being a person is the activity of meaning–making."* (ibid., p 11, emphasis ours)

An infant six months old can spot anxiety in a parent the instant he or she enters the room (Sullivan, 1957). Further, the infant then "catches" the anxiety him or her self. This is something most of us know from experience, but may have repressed. As a child, I become skilled at "reading" my parents and others. What I am reading are the signals, many of them invisible, that are emanating from another that, together with the signals emanating from me, make up a "field". The positive or negative charge of that field will determine the quality of interaction between us - whether it is collaborative and building, or competitive and defensive.

The infant, demonstrating its genius, develops an early warning system that appraises situations for possible threat. This "Foresight Function", as Sullivan labelled it, allows one to see ahead so that at an unconscious level, we know when anxiety is coming. Anxiety is such a painful experience, that early in life, this foresight allows us to substitute a more bearable emotion.

The development of defences is one of the more miraculous achievements of our unconscious minds. When those with power over us exert that power to control us, our appraisal system asks, "Does this threaten to annihilate me, render me meaningless?" The rational answer is, "Of course not!" But an infant is not a good judge of shades of "threat". At first, fear of abandonment triggers anxiety. After many experiences, the infant learns substitution. Now, *anything* that feels counter to his feelings of importance and well being triggers an appraisal of "threat!" and arouses defence. If this went uncorrected the infant would be in a constant state of anxiety. To avoid that dreadful state, the infant substitutes more moderate defensive behaviours: disagreeableness, sullenness, crying, checking out, resistance, stubbornness - the creativity is staggering.

As the infant matures, any action that ignores or threatens his need to be 'of account', to matter, will trigger some defensive manoeuvre to re-establish his meaningfulness. In effect, his action declares, "Do not fail to show me respect, I *do* matter." The underlying purpose is nothing less than *self-preservation*. These complex manoeuvres are developed *unconsciously* and with remarkable subtlety. Joseph LeDoux says, "people normally do all sorts of things for reasons they are not consciously aware of (because the behaviour is produced by brain systems that operate unconsciously) ...It seems clear that much of mental life occurs outside of conscious awareness.... We have conscious access to the outcome of the computation but not to the computation itself."

Through countless experiments the child and adult develops a complete armamentarium of defensive manoeuvres. He determines just how much defiance he can exhibit in any given situation, without retaliation. That judgement is made by his well-developed appraisal system.

One of the defensive mechanisms we use to pre-empt discounts from others is to discount ourselves! For a while, I asked each new group to write on a pad the names they called themselves when they made a mistake. The results were astounding. Everyone has a list of terrible things they called themselves, most not printable here. I wonder if, when I discount myself, some part of me gets revenge, checks out, makes mistakes, trips me up in some subtle way – and prevents me learning? After all, much of this revenge activity is unconscious.

Since we are **all** *hypersensitive to any sort of discount, we operate defensively most of the time.* Thus *anything* that limits or discourages connection–making is destructive of learning.

The implications of such a statement are staggering. It suggests that most individuals, couples and group operations work at some fraction of their possible effectiveness. It also suggests that since it is *out of conscious awareness*, no one knows it is happening (though some suspect); there are no guilty parties, and there will be no attempt to remedy the situation.

The Implications for Education

It is important that we make the field of learning as reinforcing as possible. There are forces at work in our culture that inhibit the natural impulse to learn. As parents and educators we need to know all about these "inhibitors". They are at the very core of thinking and learning. We have not seen them clearly because many of these forces are "invisible". The negative element is concealed in the positive intent that drives them. As parents and teachers we need to learn how to facilitate learning without discouraging connection-making.

Imagine a classroom where we videotape the action and stopped the tape whenever anything happened. With the tape stopped we ask, "What is going on here? Anything that might be seen as a discount?" I don't know what it would tell us, but it would identify the discount level and then we could invent some ways to reduce that level.

This opportunity is so large and complex it requires a co-ordinated approach. It is critical that teachers be thoroughly grounded in basics of thinking and learning, and the relationships that facilitate it. While this knowledge will add to their effectiveness, it is unreasonable to ask them to take on the task of teaching relationship/thinking in addition to their demanding everyday responsibilities.

I suggest that we develop a course, much like English or Mathematics, that would be taught to all students from 2nd through 9th grades. It might be called "Effective Living Skills". It would explicitly cover increasingly advanced versions of subjects such as: the connection-making process, the learning process, relationship development, creative problem solving, idea development, and the art of thinking of consequences.

The course could be developed by specialists in creative problem-solving who already have experience of working in schools, forming a team of teachers and other experts. It could be offered in existing teacher training organisations. As students become skilled in creative problem solving, they could be asked to help in reinventing education.

Would it be worthwhile? I would answer in the words of Lewis, Amini and Lannon in *A General Theory of Love* (2001) "What we do inside relationships matters more than any other aspect of human life. We conduct marriages, raise children, and organize society in whatever manner we decide. Every choice (to varying degrees) suits or flouts the heart's changeless needs."

George M. Prince is retired founder of Synectics Inc., the first creativity research company and was Chairman of the company until his retirement. He and his partners originated the idea of videotaping invention groups to learn how the process of inventing occurred. Prince published one of the early books about the process, The Practice of Creativity (Harper and Row; 1970). He has continued to investigate ways of improving group effectiveness - the interpersonal field - and recent brain research, which has emphasised the part emotions play in determining the way we deal with each other.

Victoria Logan has been a language arts teacher in the Houston Independent School district for eleven years, teaching reading and English to middle and high school students, and has also served as a lead teacher, a team leader, and a facilitator for teacher in-service training

References

Kegan, R. (1982) *The Evolving Self.* Harvard University Press, Cambridge, MA,
(1994) *In Over Our Heads, The Mental Demands of Modern Life*, Harvard University Press, Cambridge, MA
LeDoux, J.E. (1996) *The Emotional Brain*, Touchstone, New York, NY
(2002) *Synaptic Self.* Viking Penguin, New York, NY
Lewis, T; Amani, F; Lannon, R. (2000) A *General Theory of*

Love, Vintage Books, Random House, New York, NY

Sullivan, H.S. (1953) *The Interpersonal Theory of Psychiatry.* W.W. Norton, New York, NY

CREATIVITY: THE ROAD TO ENLIGHTENMENT IN EUROPEAN EDUCATION

Dr. Trevor Davies

Introduction

The central issue is that of dealing with the human condition, the spiritual and physical needs of the individual caught up within the social dynamics of reality. How can the mundane become extra-ordinary? How can stress be utilised to perform relaxation? How can human beings transcend everyday routines to achieve their potential? As Confucius said 2500 years ago:

- "Blend the best of the old with the best of the new

- Learn by doing

- Use the world as classroom

- Use music and poetry to learn and teach"

On the 6th November 2004, the Tibetan spiritual leader, the Dalai Lama called on South African educational institutions to take the lead in instilling values in society. Supported by keynote speaker, Kobus Neethling, it was argued that the 21st century needs a new kind of creativity characterised by unselfishness, caring and compassion, still involving monetary wealth but resulting in a healthy planet and healthy people. The Lisbon strategy committed Europe to becoming a world leader by 2010 in terms of the economy, educational systems and social welfare. This demands of course 'rampant creativity and innovation'. The resulting movement so far is unimpressive in all respects despite the EU having adopted the DeLors Report of 1996: 'The Four Pillars of Education for a Global Curriculum'. This agreed the following priorities:

- Learning to know, by having a broad overview of things and the skills to work in depth on selected fields; learning to learn and thereby benefit from the opportunities to learn throughout life;
- Learning to do, by acquiring vocational skills and the competencies to work in different situations and to work in teams;
- Learning to live together and appreciating other cultures and people, respecting pluralism, peace and managing conflict;
- Learning to be so as better to develop one's own personality, acting with autonomy, judgement and personal responsibility.

It has been stated by the French historian, Jacques Le Goff, that Europe's main raw material is unquestionably its grey matter. However, I recently undertook an Internet search based on keywords 'creativity' and 'Europe'; 475 sites were listed, the top three were about Korea, Taiwan and Mongolia. A search based on keywords 'creativity', 'Europe' and 'education' resulted in 59 sites being listed; the top three were from Jamaica, UK and Israel. So is the 'grey matter' of Europe engaged in appropriate ways? We are increasingly hearing the word creativity used in educational contexts and schemes developed to teach and promote it. We need to ponder for a moment and consider the implications of what this means in terms of the values, cultures and mechanisms that need to be in place in our society and in educational institutions in order to realise creative potential. Handy (1999), in his study of twenty-nine 'interesting and original individuals' whom he terms 'the new alchemists' offers advice for those involved with young peoples' education. He suggests that: "we make a great mistake if we believe that what happens in school is the main determinant of our future" (p. 47). However, he comments that:

> "Childhood experiences, wherever they occur, establish patterns of thought and behaviour, which forms deep roots. Early responsibility as a small child, the chance to test one's curiosity by experiment, to learn that mistakes

are not fatal and that change can be exciting – stifle them and you risk stunting the creative potential of the young child. Unfortunately, fearful of the dangers of modern society, children today are often over-cosseted, particularly in big cities....there is often nothing left to experimental youngsters, except computer games in the security of their own homes." (p. 47)

Creativity has become a 'buzz-word' of our times, but is often misconstrued, misunderstood and plainly misused. This implies a lack of wisdom in discussing a term that is often closely associated with wisdom. The definition can never be perceived as a product or an outcome, it is a process that people find difficult to describe, including seminal minds, but it affects us all. "Imagination rules the world" - Napoleon Bonaparte. Leaders can be catalysts but not foci and through nurturing should allow creative forces to work; to allow ideas, feelings and emotions to tumble out and to harness the potential for change that these opportunities present. This chapter explores ways in which creative potential can be promoted and harnessed through building relationships in schools, managing risk, developing values and building learning cultures.

A model of creativity for educational settings

A creative act, by its very nature must involve doing something that leads to a novel outcome or approach. There is strong agreement between writers such as Koestler, Csikzentmihalyi, Gardner and others that creativity denies simple definition and measurement, for there are many agencies that act as stakeholders in its identification. Creative acts can involve:

- using imagination, often to make unusual connections or see unusual relationships between objects, ideas or situations often from across different fields of knowledge;
- having opportunities and reasons for working which are capable of resulting in new purposes being discovered and motivation being developed;
- being comparatively original in relation to the work of

a small closed community, such as peers or family, or uniquely original in comparison with those working historically or currently in a field or discipline;
- judging value, which demands critical evaluation and reflection, standing back and gaining an overview position.

Valued creativity is usually associated with the creator striving to ensure that their knowledge in the creative field is well founded as well as searching for novel connections. Happy accidents of discovery can however sometimes occur. The following model (Figure 1) is an organising frame for creative work in education and sets out some of the issues and factors for consideration in the contexts of teaching and learning.

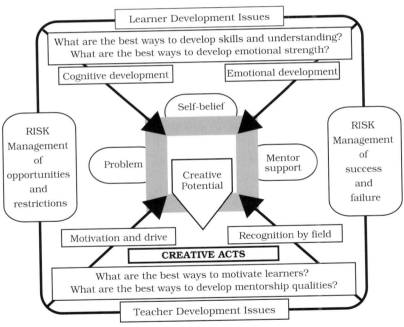

Figure 1:   *Issues in creative teaching and learning*

Cognitive and affective issues are identified and methodological questions associated with teaching and learning and the relationships between them are raised. As creativity is a very human construct, explanations for its manifestations and consequences are thought to lie firmly in the social and cultural circumstances that pervade life and living. There are many areas where teachers need to be empowered to use professional judgement and take risks in order to plan and implement meaningful experiences for learners, including creating a climate for them to take risks. There is evidence to suggest that successful risk-taking results in confident, analytical, positive students able to take decisions for themselves, even able to make judgements about the appropriateness of their teacher's advice. This is of course providing that they have a strong professional basis themselves on which to base their judgements. As Aristotle so aptly phrased: "We are what we repeatedly do. Excellence then, is not an act, but a habit".

Richard Dawkins in 'A Devil's Chaplain' enthuses after reading H G Wells's biography of his old school's famous Head, 'Sanderson of Oundle'. Sanderson's passionate desire was to give his boys freedom to fulfil themselves. He kept doors unlocked at all times to ensure that his pupils could work on their research projects. It is even reported that on finding a pupil in the school library in the early hours of one morning, he spent an hour with him talking about metallurgical processes, discovery and the values of discovery rather than sending him to bed. He also talks of Sanderson's contempt for public examinations, even though Oundle did well at them, as it was the leading school for science and technology education in his day. The values of trust are implicit in his core educational message. To strive towards excellence, new cultures have to be built that hold trust in the most central and highest regard, with all of the attendant difficulties in achieving this. This call is consistent with a desire to develop a culture that nurtures real social and cultural freedom, not one that claims freedom for markets at the expense of suppressing the richness of human diversity and creative endeavour. Above all with our learners we need to recognise the following:

- The more emotion is attached to an experience the more memorable it becomes;

- Children learn most effectively when their emotions are engaged;
- Feeling that something is right is the best way of validating our learning through knowing what we know;
- Positive emotional states are crucial in learning – emotions are the driving forces of learning.

Social and economic changes set the pace and drive for cultural developments that then become reflected in personal and social values, in attitudes, and in behaviours. Creativity in organisational, social, and intellectual contexts is increasingly recognised as the key to a prosperous future and the preparation for this begins with formal and informal education. This makes it crucial that if we really want to improve schools in a sustainable way, the managers of the change (teachers in schools) have such tools as are necessary to use flexibly and with empowerment to promote the values and beliefs associated with their particular change. Any structures created must exist in a way that support and promote changes in the learning, including associated professional development for the staff. So much change in recent decades has been undertaken for efficiency purposes but:

"There is nothing so wasteful as doing with great efficiency that which doesn't need to be done at all" (Anon)

Something that is easy to relate to is the very public question whether standards have really risen during recent times. It is not uncommon for schools to be blamed for falling standards that present excuses for 'political take-overs' of educational provision and the deskilling of teachers, but:

"To blame school for the rising tide of mediocrity is to confuse symptoms with disease. Schools can rise no higher than the expectations of the communities that surround them." (Anon)

You cannot change those expectations in society without training teachers as leaders and then empowering them to lead in and through classrooms.

Developing creative climates and cultures in European schools

Between 2001 and 2003, one-week long in-service development courses were run by the University of Reading in the locations of Krakow, Poland; Norberg, Sweden; Drammen, Norway and Ancona, Italy. They were centred on 'Learning to Learn: building structures for developing educational autonomy and creativity'. School managers and teachers working at schools and colleges ranging from pre-school to tertiary and further education attended from eleven different European countries. Post-course developments in creativity at the members' schools were followed-up one year after completion of the course through delivery of a three-part, small-scale research study. This involved 1) a questionnaire to all previous attendees; 2) a second questionnaire or telephone interview; 3) a collection of case study material as indicators of creative endeavour.

The study indicated that:

- More emphasis needs to be placed on effective, creative leadership and vision-building;
- The curricula in too many countries is content-heavy accompanied by rigid time-tabling and demands 'excessive conformity';
- Programme requirements are too restrictive and lessons are dull and boring - the topics of little interest to the learners. Pupils need opportunities to have some input into lesson planning;
- The emphasis is too excessively weighted on 'core' subjects, and arts are often squeezed to extinction;
- Fear of schools, and especially of examinations, is throttling the ability of pupils to think freely and feel free;
- Curriculum enrichment is often minimal and teachers are too pressurised to follow-up worthwhile lines of investigation and enquiry and the depth of learning experience is minimised;
- There is little attempt to assess creativity in a formative way;
- Too much concern for the performance of the school rather than the performance of the learners;

- Too little 'creative collaborative work' between teachers and learners;
- Thinking time for teachers and learners is not respected – neither have 'space' for creative activity;
- Creative work is not rewarded.

One very special Headteacher of a Special School in Surrey, UK described in passionate terms why he believed that creativity was the foundation stone of any person's individual identity in a paper he presented at a course in Ancona, Italy. The Special School's environment, through its concentrated focus on individual needs, should offer a meaningful enrichment of the student's individual horizons. The restrictions of special needs can cripple the spirit as well as impede the fulfilment of goals. Fear of ridicule, failure and plummeting self-esteem are all factors that the skilful teacher will circumnavigate, dissipate and sometimes just ignore. A key factor in creativity is the relationship between sensitive understanding and emotional support to respond to the inadequacies that make up the individual as a unique member of the human race. This same Headteacher is involved in a project with the Globe Theatre, London. His pupils perform on the stage - a Mecca of Shakespearean culture - with the dignity of any great actor.

Teachers from a number of Swedish schools in Vastmanland have attended courses on the production of movies. They learned how to create drama, soap opera and other genres of filmmaking using simple techniques. They work with their children generating storyboards, characters and backgrounds for the development of animated film based on their lives, folklore and culture. These are often used in international projects including France, England, Poland, Italy and Denmark. One primary school has developed a close relationship with a school in Zimbabwe. Children and teachers exchange letters and visits. A booklet has been produced for the children in each country to learn each other's languages through discussing common themes and topics. The mission is to achieve common understanding and values through defeating ignorance that in so many ways blights relationships across nationalities and cultures in modern societies.

The findings from this work were triangulated with a recent European Commission survey of a very successful project series, Comenius 1, which is based on groups of schools from across Europe coming together into partnerships to undertake exchanges and innovative curriculum and extra-curricular work. 10,000 schools across Member and Associated States were involved at the time of the survey and responses from 1398 schools across all phases of schooling were analysed. The results illustrate how powerful innovative opportunities and freedom for teachers and schools can be. It details the benefits of schools working in cross-cultural settings. Strong features of this major programme include:

* The role of international projects as catalysts for innovation;
* Recognition that involvement in projects helps teachers to develop their teaching methods in more creative ways and that active support from senior managers in schools is essential to successful creative activity. This inevitably entails changes to the structure, culture and values of schools, ones that are needed to provide the conditions for a better curriculum for learning and pedagogy for learning.
* Comenius 1 is used as a vehicle for implementing major educational change in many countries. The experience of a Romanian Lycée, for instance, demonstrated that a school involved in a series of dynamic and highly motivating transnational projects is best placed to achieve effective change.

Participants see the European dimension in education as critical in engendering a school-wide culture of imaginative and creative learning, namely, 'thinking outside the box'. The opportunities presented by international projects re-enforce the role of the 'teacher as a learner', that is critical to managing change in their own classrooms. In a climate where schools have become much more subject to following directives from politicians and receiving resources directly for 'politically approved activities' there is greater reluctance on behalf of many teachers to 'go beyond their brief'. Hence stimulating interest and involvement demands much more persuasive leadership as distinct from a managerial approach where decisions are dispensed efficiently. If we are to create common European identities that are based on trust, common value systems must be built where common interests are developed but divergent interests are tolerated and even celebrated.

I met two years ago (2003), a newly appointed Headteacher to a new 'Academy' school in Georgia, USA that had not yet begun to be designed; 2006 was then (and still is) the target time for opening. But guess what, he was leading a team to develop a new school concept that was research-led, not simply implementing traditional rules and formulae. Trust was to be the central platform for this new school amongst the founding principles. Many are recognisable and even universal concerning the development of high standards and achievement, even education of the 'whole person', but others were more interesting:

- Teachers focus on higher levels of thinking, learning and supporting students to apply skills and knowledge
- Students are excited about classes, arriving promptly and seldom missing sessions
- Academies and courses are structured around student interests and potential career pathways
- Teachers help students to learn "what to do when they don't know what to do"
- Teachers establish relationships with students, getting to know their interests, learning preferences and unique qualities so these can be used to better promote higher levels of understanding and achievement
- Teachers motivate and ignite student curiosity by framing curriculum around relevant and meaningful real-world projects and assignments
- Teachers work together to format instruction/curriculum to help students make "connections" between science, mathematics, social sciences, etc.
- School is changed from a place where kids come to watch old people work to a place where they are the "workers" who are challenged and move to the centre of their own

learning
- Assignments must always be legitimately designed around meaningful and relevant ends
- Teachers will no longer be just "covering" material but asked to go into depth thereby promoting deeper understanding and mastery
- Students will be encouraged to constantly challenge their teachers and the system to answer the question, "When will I ever use what you are teaching me today?" If there is not a satisfactory answer to the question it is time to reconsider that particular content or assignment
- Core academic teachers will be teaching the same students throughout their high school experience
- Hands-on, action-based projects will become common throughout the program
- Students will see an integration of subjects and disciplines
- Teachers will be required to work together with colleagues in a "teamwork" approach to teaching and learning
- Higher education and business leaders will help serve as advisors, supporters and liaisons for academies and teachers

Another central element of the Academy Model is the inclusion of a senior project. Twelfth-grade students will be required to complete a capstone project during their final semester. It is to be research-based and result in a paper, a multi-media presentation or a performance. The project would have to be both original and valuable in extending knowledge in a particular area. Presentations of projects would be made during the final weeks of the school year and adjudicated by teachers and higher education officials, along with business and community representatives.

Involving the learner in designing the future

In order to move forward and design educational provision for the future, there is a need to re-visit some fundamental questions. This is not fashionable but necessary in a bid to understand the relationship between visions for education and visions for society. These questions might include:

Nature of knowledge

- Do we know what a well-educated person should know?
- There is confusion between the nature of knowledge and the nature of information. What is their relationship and how does this affect how we view and build educational curricula?

Nature of learning

- The human brain works best in a highly stimulating, low threat environment. How do we maximise its potential?
- Learning is a social activity. To what extent is this potential being realised in schools?
- Learning is a cultural activity. To what extent is this potential being realised in schools?

For students to achieve their creative potential, an appropriate climate needs to be created and the curriculum and teaching designed to match. This could be in school and /or at home. The evidence from studies of recognised creative individuals (such as Noam Chomsky and Wolfgang Amadeus Mozart) suggests that from very early ages, they were immersed in the domains in which they were ultimately successful, in an active, language-rich, way. The results are often attributed to parentage and home life. Hence dialogue and mutual understanding between parents and teachers is required. In schools, teachers often believe that they are promoting 'interactive ideas exchange' in their classrooms. In practice, learners often disagree; they feel restricted, even inhibited, in an 'assessment driven' environment.

The 'fun factor' of working with others is important to teachers and learners. A pivotal factor of many creative people, is their ability to switch from free associative methods of thinking, to highly directed and perseverative thinking modes. All learners can be encouraged/supported to achieve this flexibility through appropriate teaching. Balancing the degree of fun and challenge in the work is considered by most learners with varying degrees of confidence to be most effective in helping them to maintain motivation and progress. Additionally, group work is an opportunity to test social techniques in a general sense: to 'try out' leadership skills through manipulating the ideas and models of others and gain influence and credibility through adopting a mixture of free and directed thinking. A major tool for the teacher is questioning; their questions and those of their pupils:

> "...fundamental to the development of better questioning skills is the teacher's ability to be respectful of the questions children ask and to help them achieve the skills for finding the answers. Nothing is more rewarding to the child who asks a question than to find the answer. This does not mean that the teacher must answer the question immediately or answer it at all."

There is a growing realisation that the locus of educational control must operate more with learning and learners than teaching and teachers. This is also consistent with recognising the need for learning to be deeper and more meaningful than 'simple' theoretical or even vocational approaches. Pedagogic leadership concentrates on the following three elements:

- Improving and leading the change of teaching;

- Improving and leading the development of teacher professionalism;

- Improving and leading teachers' reflection in relation to National Curricula and the goals of the school.

"I must create a system or be enslaved by another man's. I will not reason and compare: my business is to create." (William Blake). We need cultures in education across society that celebrates difference, develops potential and helps form strategies to build knowledge, emotional intelligence and empowerment. Social, emotional and motivational factors are important for learners and influence how they respond and perform within the domain and situation they are working in. As learners become more confident and mature they are more capable and gain the motivation to turn social situations to their advantage. We must never lose sight of each individual's intrinsic worth. It is this force that must be harnessed. Its limitations should not be set by a conforming society but by the stars of the Milky Way, as Perry Como said 50 years ago:

"catch a falling star and put it in your pocket save it for a rainy day.... Never let it fade away."

Trevor Davies is a Lecturer in Technology and Physics Education at the Institute of Education, University of Reading. Prior to that, he was the Project Director for the Six Counties Technology Project. He was previously the Deputy Headteacher of a large 11-18 comprehensive school, a Local Authority advisor and an Ofsted inspector. He has worked internationally throughout Europe for 12 years undertaking training development, evaluation and research work in education. He has also undertaken collaborative development work and research involving USA, Australia and Brazil.

He has published recently:
¨ Davies, T & Gilbert, J. (2003). Modelling: promoting creativity whilst forging links between science education and design and technology education. Canadian Journal of Science, Mathematics and Technology Education. 3 (1) University of Toronto Press: Canada.
¨ Davies, T. (2002). Creativity: its contribution to design and technology education. Unpublished Ph. D Thesis. University of Reading
t.c.davies@reading.ac.uk

REFLECTION: THINKING ABOUT YOUR EXPERIENCE OF TEACHING THINKING

By Graham Rawlinson. C.Psychol. FRSA

The relationship between teaching and learning is not so simple. We teach something in lots of different ways, and then, sometimes in ways that seem miraculous, they 'get it!' It can be a slow and painful process, and it can be magically quick. The more we try to squeeze into the curriculum the more frustrating it can become, "speed up the machine" is the cry, but the machine refuses to speed up without major accidents occurring. So Reinventing Education is about how to avoid these accidents while trying to achieve the same principle objective – has learning moved to the next level of understanding?

If we are researchers in the process of learning we ask ourselves "how did they 'get it'?", and we become a little better at helping them learn how to learn. Good teachers seem to find ways of knowing when to provide the right key for that process, but there is still no rushing it. This applies whether you are teaching adults to cook, or children to read.

So Reinventing Education for me is about changing from teaching in breadth to teaching in depth, in a deliberate way. Changing to teaching in depth requires seeing depth as the key goal, most of the time. It means moving to teaching thinking about thinking, so the teacher's task is to *think about* Thinking about Thinking. Rather than using the expression Thinking about Thinking all the time, I will substitute the expression with the word reflection, but the implication is still an active process of doing something, i.e. Thinking, about your experience of Thinking.

This often gets confused, and maybe this is confusing! Let me provide an example. If I say I am thinking about my house, I might just mean I am experiencing an image of my house in my head, it is there, and that is all. But I might also say I am thinking about my house and I mean that I am thinking about its need for decorating, as it is looking well worn in some places, and is falling apart in others, and all this thinking is coming together as I actively reflect on my house, so I am actively thinking about my thinking.

At one level teaching in breadth is easier, as everything is on the same plane. It is two dimensional. It is complex only in that there are so many things that could be taught. It is easier to test in that it is quantity that is important, but it is more difficult in that there are so many things to test.

Teaching in depth is easier in that only the essence is important, not the detail, but it is more complex in that the relationships at different depths are more difficult to picture. We are not used to representing the world as having lots of dimensions, other than space and time. But it can be easier to test depth in that demonstrating an understanding of the essence provides a lot of information all in one go. If a vet takes one look at your poorly cat, then gently pulls a leg joint back into position, the vet probably has a good understanding in depth of the essence of how a cat's joints work.

I once was trying to review how the responses by students to exam questions were embedded in the whole of the answer or were an accumulation of many specific parts. As an experiment I had looked at exam questions in electrical engineering and tried to 'guess' what the end grades would be even though I had no idea if the answers, and much of it was mathematics, were correct. Almost all the marks I gave were very close to those given by the tutor (within one or two percent), except for one paper, and I asked about that paper and the tutor admitted that he had been generous as in a previous paper the student had done so badly he was going to fail anyway!

So then I asked a tutor for English and my question was, "if I gave you just a couple of paragraphs of an essay, could you reliably mark the whole paper, and the answer was, "oh yes, you can tell who knows what they are saying and who doesn't". So tutors tend to know who knows the subject from the embedded knowledge in depth which shows all the way through the exam paper or essay!

Teaching in depth

When we teach a topic, we can ask, what is it, in essence, we wish to have people learn?

We might teach 'picture framing in 18th century Latvia', as a topic, but what we want them to learn is something about the physical craft of picture framing, something about the culture of another country in Europe, something about the history of Europe.

We might leave them to guess what it is that we wish them to learn, and too often we do. Or we can teach them also some ways of reflecting on what they see, what they hear, what they feel and what they do. And so we coach them into reflecting on the key issues we see as important. What comes out of the reflection is an understanding of the topic in depth.

Understanding in depth means:
1. Understanding that *things out there are as they are* which is not how they appear, the map is not the terrain
2. That the way they seem to us reflects in part *what kind of lenses we use to see* them and how we use these lenses to create maps of our own understanding
3. How we see things reflects *what kind of looking* we are applying, which is something about reflecting on ourselves and our seeing; what I find on the map reflects what I am looking for, my purpose.
4. How I see things links to *how others see things* through understanding the tools they are using for seeing things and the purpose others have for looking.

This kind of thinking about teaching and learning is not new. And it applies not just to children but to adults too. We know that. But how do we teach reflecting about thinking?

Developing levels of reflection and through reflection gaining deeper understanding

1. Things as they are

Reflecting in depth on *things as they are* requires a process of exploring different levels. A medal as a piece of jewellery is a on a different *plane*, from a medal as an award or a medal as a sign of authority.

Making sense of the world out there is not just what is there but how it relates to the context in which it sits, and contexts exist at different levels.

So 'picture framing', for example, exists within the context of our understanding of technology and science at one level, in the context of our understanding of community and society at another level, and at the development of the relationship between science and technology and the development of communities at an even deeper level.

Some of this thinking may be seen as systems thinking, but not all systems are directly linked, so we cannot always have a clear hierarchy of one level to another. This kind of thing makes writing software programmes difficult! And in the same way it makes thinking about complex systems difficult, e.g. ideas about society, family and crime.

So teaching reflecting about thinking means being realistic about how some things are connected and other things are not so connected. And the differences are real, so how things are is often not reducible to a single, simple way of thinking about what is real and not real.

And teaching this kind of reflection means that the learner makes a connection between how they think things are and what lenses they are using to see things.

2. Lenses

Learners can learn to reflect on how we use lenses to magnify a picture, zoom in, to look at the detail. They can learn how we zoom out, to see the bigger picture. And they can learn how we filter in order to see only what we wish to see and leave out things that will confuse us.

We can use creative lenses as well as physical or analytical lenses. We can imagine we are very small and want to move around through the hairs of our dog. What would we find?

We can change an image so that we only see in black and white, or only in red, or only in squares. We can give the learners experience of doing this, and then we get them to imagine it, so they are not reliant on the physical experience.

We can get them to imagine things are connected and ask what difference that would make. We can get them to change features in their imagination and ask how that might change what happens next.

And when they have explored for a little while how different uses of lenses affects how they see things, then we can link this to asking why they are looking, and what the link is between how they are looking and why they are looking, what purpose they have.

3. Ways of Looking

We have different purposes for looking and thinking and these will link in different ways to how we are looking.

We can look with clear purpose, looking to find something, and as soon as we see it we will know we have found it, or at least be sure we are on the right path. This is science work, science thinking, or we may say it is detective work.

We can look to explore, to build experience, to find the unexpected.

What we want to do may affect how we want to look, and the opposite is true, how we are looking may affect what we think we are looking for.

And when we have experienced for a while how we can look in different ways, we can look, through our imaginations or by role playing, at different ways of looking, how others may see things differently, and how we might communicate these differences.

4. How others see things

The most sophisticated learning occurs when the learner realises that they can reflect on how others see things in different ways because the world can be seen in different ways, how the world may not have a single reality, how the world looks differently depending on what lenses you use and what purposes you have for looking.

This kind of learning is often seen as a core part of the process of learning at undergraduate and postgraduate levels, but perhaps this is because we do not trust our younger or less sophisticated learners to do this, and we do not give them the tools for reflecting in this way.

One way to assist this process of reflecting on how others see things, how others think about things, is to give them inquiry tools which are not confrontational and which do not lead to a sense of who is right and who is wrong. So we avoid asking "why do you think that?" which can lead to feeling questioned about the rightness of how you think, but ask instead, having said, "mmmmmm – interesting", "tell me more about how you see this thing this way".

Processes for aiding reflection

Effective thinking, effective reflection, comes from using both analytical thinking and creative thinking, using all our brain and parts of our brain, in an iterative way. Using our 'art' and our 'science' is essential for developing learners' ability to learn in depth.

Fortunately, we have more modern tools than Socratic Dialogue and Rhetoric. We can use creative thinking tools such as lateral thinking, or Synectics, or TRIZ, and we can use analytical thinking tools such as TRIZ, or even Finite Element Analysis for something really technical. We can use Synectics processes for communication in groups, so that we help learners listen to what others say, we help them share their view, we help them build their picture and in an open way invite them to see our different picture(s)

We can uses processes like Appreciative Inquiry, or more analytically, Soft Systems Analysis to build more complex pictures of how many different people see things in many different ways.

Teaching in depth

Teaching in depth is not necessarily doing that much that is that different, as all learners need lots of experience, to build their understanding through experience. The final part of that well known phrase is, "I do and I understand".

Teaching in depth, helping learners to learn in depth, is about applying processes to assist those leaps forward, about making sure that the depth is the most critical part of the movement forward, that learners do come with different learning styles so some may need different ways of getting it in depth, but the getting it is the most important thing, not the method of getting it.

We can help learners by learning ourselves how to use these processes, at least some of them. We can plan our teaching so that we make sure we are helping them with those processes, and we can plan to check how well the learners are gaining an understanding of those 4 parts of learning in depth:

1. Understanding that things out there are as they are which is not how they appear, the map is not the terrain - how do we engage the learner in an enquiry into the relationship between the map and the terrain?

We might, for example, use analogous situations where we help them see this difference. We might use physical maps produced for different purposes, those for road systems compared to maps of agriculture, or we might look at newspaper stories as maps of the terrain of an event, and ask how the different maps all carry some feature of reality but not all features, only the real terrain carries all the features.

2. That the way they seem to us reflects in part *what kind of lenses, we use to see* them, and how we use these lenses to create maps of our own understanding

The lenses may be physical devices of course, from glass lenses to standard measuring instruments, but they may also be surveys, artistic renderings, poetic discourse. The learner can learn from examples, again examples outside the immediate field are useful to help them get the generic point, that the tools they are using to examine something are themselves part of the creation of the picture, the representation.

3. How we see things reflects *what kind of looking* we are applying, which is something about reflecting on ourselves and our seeing, what I find on the map reflects what I am looking for, my purpose.

We ask the student what they might be looking for, why are they looking? One way to do this is to actually video the student talking about what they are looking for and how they are looking. They can then reflect, with guidance and help, on what they are saying. Or the work produced by the learner can invite specific responses to what they are saying. So if the student is saying they are looking for trends in manufacturing across Europe, the reflective question could be, "what might yield observation of these different trends?" Do you have an outcome you are looking for, and if so, might you find something simply because you are looking for it?

It is necessary to understand the Bayesian approach to enquiry, that before you can say you have 'evidence' supporting a hypothesis you need to ask yourself how many other ways of getting that evidence there might be. How many other hypotheses are there which would lead you to see what you see even though what you wish to conclude may be based on an error in making too few hypotheses in the first place. If you are determined enough, you will find what you are looking for, whether it is there or not.

4. How I see things links to *how others see things* through understanding the tools they are using for seeing things and the purpose others have for looking.

The learner is to be encouraged to see things from different perspectives, whether we are talking about race and gender, or simply trying to understand the way communities of ants behave. It is helpful to use strong imagination processes to help this process of seeing things from different perspectives. One field which does this well is Biomimetics, the study of natural things from a technical solution point of view. For example, a leaf is a fantastic device for delivering unfolding and has some of the best origami you can imagine. But to understand this you need to zoom in, to see things from an entirely different scaling, to imagine yourself a molecule and what is pushing and pulling you around. The TRIZ process encourages this imagination of the small and large, to enable the learner, the investigator, to realise that their model is not the only model, that there are many models and the learning comes from understanding how all these models help to build the bigger picture.

We need to understand that a learner may fully understand all four in one field of learning but not apply them at all to another, so we need to check with them, if this is true, how they are seeing the world in less depth at times. I might fully understand all four parts when I reflect on people's political preferences and viewpoints, but not be able to understand how they can like stewed cabbage. Or I might fully understand people's dietary preferences, but have no idea how they can think of voting as they do.

So to reinvent education, maybe our checklist should include, for each field of study:

How do I teach, and how do they learn, and how do I check this?

Using Stephen Covey's idea, "begin with the end in mind", and valuing self managed learning, we can facilitate this by helping the learners manage this themselves.

In simple summary, which in itself is a map not the terrain, we help the learner by helping them to ask themselves:

1. Have I understood the field as it is, out there, in that kind of reality?
2. Do I understand how the way I am looking at it is affecting how I see it?
3. Do I understand why I am looking, for what purpose?
4. How do others see things?

And if this is a way of developing our understanding in many different fields, maybe it will help some other great objectives, like developing citizenship, developing sustainable technologies, developing co-operative and creative communities.

It is often said, and 'proved' by the expansion of stores of information, that the knowledge we have is growing exponentially. If we are to manage this growth in knowledge without creating the accidents, where knowledge is like too many trains running along too poor an infrastructure, we must be smart, we must look to Reinventing Education as learning in depth, a mastery of process of accessing and using knowledge not of storing it in our heads. We need to be thinking about thinking about thinking.

All comments welcome to Graham@partnershipswork.co.uk

Credit for my thinking about thinking goes to the great book by Robert Kegan, In Over Our Heads, Mental Demands of Modern Life (Harvard University Press 1995) amongst too many others to name.

TRIZ can be explored in many books, from Darrell Mann, Hands on Systematic Thinking, (Creax Press 2002) to Ellen Domb, Simplified TRIZ, (St Lucie Press 2002).

Graham Rawlinson is the author of "How to Invent (Almost) Anything", "Choices" and "The No Recipe Cookbook". Expert innovation consultant and facilitator with companies round the world using Synectics and TRIZ, (Theory of Inventive Problem Solving). Founder member of the BPS Coaching Psychology Group, founding Chair of his Local Rural Inventors Club, Fellow of the RSA.

CHANGING EDUCATION: CURRICULA AND BRAIN EXPERIMENTS

Harry Forster

Education tomorrow may be better for a variety of reasons: there could be a new curriculum that has been established by a central authority, with standards and assessments that enforce those standards.

Computers could be involved in all phases of the education process and everyone could be connected. Schools could be restructured for more local control; teachers and students could interact at a distance. Privatisation and globalisation may provide new opportunities for change. Learning modules could be assembled into courses that are protected by Digital Rights Management systems. Student and teacher blogs, Wikis and social software could contribute to group interaction and co-operative learning.

All of the above may be parts of the future but none of them get to the heart of the problem of education – What is learning? Learning is a brain centred process. "...facts about the brain allowed me to answer questions that seemed unanswerable using purely behavioural measures" Stephen M. Kosslyn

The better you can describe what you are doing in terms of what the student's brain is doing, the more likely you will succeed. This perspective creates entirely new ways of viewing each of the above ideas for the improvement of education. How does a new administrative system relate to a brain oriented education system? How does a new delivery medium facilitate the brain processes of learning? Does that new law facilitate or limit the mechanisms of education?

Technology has brought us many new feasibilities. Computer and communication power will be massive. Applications that we would not allow our minds to think of previously will be commonplace. New educational administrative, assessment, and delivery systems using these powers will be implemented. The challenge is to remember that though man has drastically advanced his ability to control nature, the nature of man is essentially unchanged. We can build aircraft whose performance exceeds man's ability to fly them - they must be controlled by computers.

In a similar way the next education system will have to be driven by computers. Education systems that depend on graphics and include brain models and brain-oriented data will be like the aircraft - the backbone will be electronic communication and assistance.

The concept of a brain-oriented education system is growing rapidly. The Organisation for Economic Co-operation and Development (OECD) has recently (July 2002) created the Directorate for Education (1) with a Learning Sciences and Brain Research website (2). They describe the site as follows:

" This space is for teaching practitioners from all levels, forms and places of education and learning. Our vision is that you will use it to address in your own terms and according to your own priorities the challenge of belonging to an occupation at the leading edge of scientific, professional and technological development.
In particular, we hope the space will offer an opportunity for you to discuss, freely and openly, issues and experiences about the brain and its role in the process of learning that relate to your own involvement in education. Teaching practitioners today are at the epicentre of far-reaching changes in many key aspects of formal education."

Within this website are the Brain and Learning (3) TeachtheBrain Forums where this discussion can take place.

George P. Lakoff, professor of linguistics at the University of California, Berkeley, introduces the concept of the "embodied" mind in which almost all of human cognition depends on brain facilities such as the sensorimotor system and the emotions. (http://en.wikipedia.org/wiki/Embodied_philosophy)

Working in the context of the brain leads to massively complex systems of thought and voluminous amounts of data to process. This induces two new characteristics of the future education system. The content of the curriculum has to reflect new knowledge about the brain and how to handle information with new computer tools and new computing power. We have to move to teaching people how to handle more complex and extensive problems than those that the present curriculum is developed for. Computer systems will be harnessed to aid us in delivering and assessing education.

Two Paradigms

As an example of the type of new thinking that is required to bring us closer to a brain-oriented educational system, look at the traditional conception of an educational situation as shown in Illustration 1. The student is presented with a problem to solve. He/she has some intuitive model (sometimes called an informal, tacit, or implicit model) in their mind as to what the problem presented is. This model has been created and/or triggered by some form of linguistic communication that has a semantic structure. This communication causes the brain to link to a strategy for answering or solving the problem. The solution strategies are related to how the student sees the problem (the model). Each of these pieces is perceived as intellectual ideas outside of the mind. They are generally assumed to exist in the curriculum, the text, and the teaching philosophy. All of the elements relate to the brain but they are external to it as shown in Illustration 1. This is a form of disembodied philosophy as opposed to the embodied philosophy that follows.

The new thinking says that you should look first to the brain/mind world (bmw) complex when you want to develop curriculum, apply technology, or administer education. This complex is where knowledge and understanding are created through education and manipulated through human actions. The use of the complex is facilitated by a framework of how this complex works. The question is where the components of the disembodied model could be located in the bmw complex?

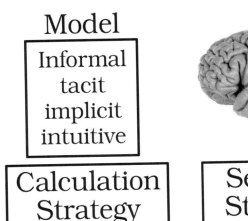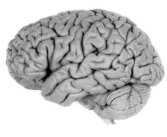

Illustration 1 A Disembodied Traditional Educational Conceptual Structure

They are most likely in the associative cortex which is the thin wrinkled covering of the brain. It is known that specific brain activities are localised in specific regions of the brain. The syntactic structure is a linguistic structure which would mean that it would likely be centred in the region were language functions are located. This could be in the areas of the brain where we find the Broca and Wernicke speech areas shown in Illustration 2.

Solution strategies are plans for action. Planning is generally associated with the frontal lobe located at the front of the brain on the left of the illustration. An intuitive model is an association of concepts that are stored in the brain. Brain research has shown that concept structures are spread in complex patterns throughout the associative cortex. We are still talking about the same ideas as traditional thinking except that we have placed them in a new context – the physiology of the brain and neural system.

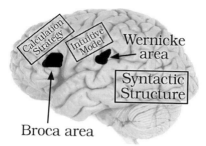

Illustration 2 Brain Areas Corresponding to Traditional Educational Conceptual Structures

Curricula and Brain

A more complete set of brain function localisations is shown in Illustration 3. If one were to adopt the ideas of Illustrations 2 and 3, how would this be reflected in a new curriculum and delivery system? Fortunately some excellent work has already been done by Professor Dr.Uwe Multhaup (4) Illustration 3 is taken from the materials he uses to teach future language teachers. He describes the type of information on brain structure and brain operation that is put into the new curricula and also how the theory of brain function relates to the learning process. Throughout the site he describes how brain processing relates to various teaching styles.

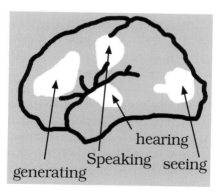

Illustration 3 Brain Function Localization

What does it mean to create a new model of this nature? It could be argued that there is nothing new. There is still an intuitive model, a syntactic structure, and a calculation strategy and all we have is a new illustration. It is my contention that for intellectual matters the closer your thinking comes to being based on the brain and brain function the more likely you will have better understanding. This new context is a step in the direction of Dr. Kosslyn. As Professor Multhaup demonstrates, the new model facilitates the incorporation of other knowledge. If a teacher is having difficulty with a student, Illustration 3 provides many new things to think about. You can also bring in ideas such as metaphors of Lakoff, brain scan data and cognitive science of William Calvin, and the linguistics of Chomsky. Professor Kosslyn's idea that facts about the brain allows answers that seemed unanswerable using purely behavioural measures, takes on a new significance.

Experiments

I used this type of thinking to teach a brain handicapped student to read. He was in the seventh grade and could not read the word "a". The traditional education system had worked with him for seven years and had completely failed. Within months we had him reading.

The ideas are not limited to language. I have also applied this to mathematics. A 19 year old student in the traditional education system is not allowed past the third grade level due to traditional thinking and curricula. When he was 16 I used a graphical technique that represents the logic of math and algebra to test if the student could mentally understand the concepts of algebra. In less than three hours the student created the graph of the assets portion of a balance sheet. This graphic represents not only algebraic computation but also the solution of a set of simultaneous equations. The student set up the problem, inserted values from his life experience, and solved the entire problem.

In problems of this nature there are three types of knowledge. The first is concept knowledge or understanding of what a thing is. The second is logical knowledge or understanding of how concepts are related and the third is process knowledge or understanding of how to operate on the concepts subject to the logic of the problem to obtain a result. These are all different classes of brain functions.

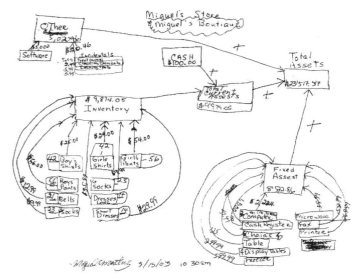

Illustration 4 Student representation of Total Assets

In the graphical assessment technique each of these brain capacities is separated so that it is possible better to evaluate what a student can and cannot do.

Dennis Lomas of the *Ontario Institute for Studies in Education, University of Toronto* looked at graphical techniques in education because of their ease of use in the new computer world of education. He shows that graphical reasoning goes back to Socrates. "Socrates' theory of learning as 'remembering,' a sort of innateness claim: There is no teaching but recollection'" (5)

Lomas says, " diagrammatic reasoning is not just an intuitive tool, but a full-fledged part of some types of mathematical reasoning." He concludes " Thus mathematical diagrams play two interrelated roles in mathematical thought, 1) as objects that people attempt to extract implicit information from, and 2) as representations of classes of geometric shapes to which reasoning applies. Both these elements are indispensable in the reasoning itself."

Additional materials on these subjects can be found at http: //207.30.247.157:8080/beaulieu

Harry Forster has moved between industry and academia. He started in defence electronics where he was awarded many patents for his work. He then moved into military operations and systems analysis with small consulting groups. Subsequently, he became an instructor and professor in electronics and computer software. He authored and co-authored texts on mathematics for electronics including one that is now in its 8th edition.

He has studied brain processing, scanning techniques, cognitive science, neuroanatomy, linguistics and the brain. He started a tutoring program where he had the opportunities to do the work reported in this article.

References

(1) http://www.oecd.org/department/0,2688,en_2649_33723 _1_1_ 1_1_1,00.html
(2) http://www.teachthebrain.org/
(3) http://www.teachthebrain.org/forums/forumdisplay.php?f=17
(4) Illustration 3 is taken from the materials Professor Dr. Uwe Multhaup uses to teach future language teachers. In his teachings he shows how the new paradigm affects the teaching and learning process. He also uses it to show how and why present curricula fail. This is a very practical demonstration of the new brain oriented teaching. To learn more about his technique go to his website at http://www2.uniwuppertal.de/ FB4/anglistik/multhaup/ (There are materials in both English and German)
(5) A transcript of the interaction with Socrates can be found in " The History of Mathematics, A Reader", p61, edited by John Fauvel and Jeremy Gray. The dialogue starts with Meno the

slave boy saying, "What do you mean when you say that we don't learn anything, but that what we call learning is recollection?"

i   Diagrams in Mathematical Education: A Philosophical Appraisal, Dennis Lomas *Ontario Institute for Studies in Education,* University of Toronto
http://www.ed.uiuc.edu/EPS/PESyearbook/1998/lomas.html

NOURISHING THE SPECIAL NEEDS OF EVERY CHILD

Christopher Gilmore

Education has always been incremental, so I have included in my proposals what is already evolving. Personalised education and learning still prosper in many forms. Increasingly, it could be said to be the way forward.

Too often the power remains in the hands of politicians, who will have their own way despite democratic protests. State-imposed school rules too often curtail the voice of the individual teacher, parent and child. Imposed education is systemised bullying. Around 20 school fires a week suggest a reaction fuelled by pupil power.

From 1988, the year the national curriculum was introduced in UK, the boast has been maintained that it provides a broad and balanced curriculum. Yet politicians of all parties are complaining that it is too prescriptive, too stressful and lacks flexibility. These worries were reported in April 2005 in the Times Educational Supplement. Interestingly, it contained 80 pages of news and views against 172 pages advertising jobs! Hardly an indication that all is well in a healthy education system.

There is a missing link. My plea is "let all educators and their clients facilitate more fully the basic and perennial needs of the human personality".

Encouragingly, the Education Secretary has expressed her desire for both a 'creative curriculum' and for 'flexibility'. And to give the Government due praise, its primary strategy is already providing some release from the constraints of its earlier literacy and numeracy directives. But how long in secondary education before such aspirations create a firm but flexible framework for personalised education?

Adults in positions of political power sometimes change things more quickly when the established system no longer feeds the needs of their own status as leaders. In these heady times of transition, the media challenges us all with real-life headlines like:

- Dropout rate hits 100,000 in UK schools
- Attacks on teachers rise to one a day
- Increase in playground bullying

Is it not feasible that when pupils so often feel hopeless, the most effective way to show any personal power, to feel 'special', is to rebel? Resistance to authority can take the form of passive apathy, and/or become pro-actively self-destructive, as in drug abuse. In prisons as in city streets, anger can explode into riots. Of course, in states of emergency, the Government can bring in Special Powers. The country's overcrowded jails, like school classrooms, are full of inmates who have educational Special Needs. Whatever the circumstances, the human fact is that every single person, of all ages, wishes to feel SPECIAL. This is the Number One requirement for self-esteem.

But a school class system based on constant measuring, with a regular stress on standards as standardisation, cannot nourish more specialised aspirations. This prescriptive curriculum should carry a Government Health Warning, just as doctors' medical prescriptions carry a warning as to their possible side effects (including those on Ritalin, now used so widely to tranquillise non-compliant kids).

Can the best of personal powers be freed into self-expression in any academic institution with a traditional bureaucratic infrastructure? According to headteacher Derek Wise, they can. 'I want to de-institutionalise the school so that students feel they're there as a person, not as a herd.'

In his comprehensive school, he plans to inaugurate university-type lectures; install a cloakroom attendant in the toilets; provide large halls for the students in break times and in all ways treat the schoolchildren with respect. Further, students will be encouraged to take charge of their own learning by learning how to learn, coached by a dedicated counsellor. How deep into self-development such innovations will go remains vague. To teachers dedicated to traditional timetables, tackling a roll of 1,600 students, the prospect of widespread student-centred approaches must threaten a bureaucratic nightmare. The complementary strategies I'm about to propose might save this bold vision from falling short of its life-enhancing potential.

Wise intends his school to use accelerated learning techniques together with a study of the learning styles that best suits each individual. All students will have the back-up of the latest technology to hone the skills needed for independent learning, and also those that create a cohesive community of learners. The school is in the new town, Cramlington, 12 miles from Newcastle-upon-Tyne. It is a good start and is being well supported by the Specialist Schools Trust.

Five 'Directives'

David Miliband, when schools minister, set out ways of loosening the straitjacket of the present national curriculum without, significantly, losing regular testing. Diagnostically, he stated that a personalised learning scheme must consider the following five components.

First, 'Teachers must know the strengths and weaknesses of individual students.'

Not students themselves? This approach seems staff-centred. Better, surely, to provide strategies for students to define themselves through direct experiences; learning through making personal choices and monitoring their consequences; a form of bespoke goal setting and goal scoring as in Personal Profiling

Second, 'Helped by the recognition of multiple intelligences and different learning styles, educational strategies must stretch each student ... by creatively deploying teachers and ICT.'

This assumes that teachers are not too weary to obey the order to be 'creative'. After years of strangulating paperwork, most may now be too entrenched in their own style of school subject delivery. Anyway, most youngsters know more about computers than many adults. How about a community of shared learners?

Third, 'Curriculum choice must be offered, especially post-14 but also through curriculum-enhancing activities in earlier phases.'

Yet in current circumstances, key stage 3 is so poorly funded. Secondary school is often too late for children to recover enough confidence to make autonomous choices if, in their primary years, they have not been offered such exciting opportunities. School staff, after years of timetabling and obediently complying with state-imposed dictates, are likely to find threatening the challenge of these more flexible changes. In my proposal, creative and trusted teachers would already be flexible enough to facilitate the vagaries of human variety in any number of complementary ways. Already, Circle Times, used sensitively, serve as a preliminary form of self-profiling, encouraging a collegiate open honesty all round.

Fourth, 'Head teachers must find more radical ways in which to organise all school activities as well as a more flexible use of support staff.'

Yet school years have limited time to hit targets and steer expected numbers of students into university. Since the Government has not released the system from GCSE, AS and A2 exam requirements, there is a discrepancy between the proposed personalised learning modes and the older 'mug-an-jug' competitive methods that have led to the alarmist newspaper headlines quoted above. Hence my complementary approach

Miliband again. 'Links must be forged with local groups and social services, all contacts to encourage more partnerships within the community at large.'

No complaints there. Not that is, until Mr Smith and Mrs Jones complain that their respective children are enjoying themselves so much on their chosen interest, they neglect the 3Rs. A lifeline as a passion, be it Mr Smith's teenage son and his love of designing kites; or Mrs Jones' teenage daughter's fascination for collecting fossils, is better found in teenage years than never. With hormones arriving, hobbies like fashions, can become an obsession that can drive the passionate student away from schooling before the academic basics are sufficiently mastered. So what?

The Making of Me

Better that young children, in their earliest years, collect uplifting praise from adults for activating their own pet interests. By expressing their special gifts, children can so be encouraged, developmentally, to grow into them. Self-worth so established, such talents could become integrated with the business of learning the basics. In such dedicated kids, one can recognise a certain central steadiness, be it because they are committed to mucking out ponies, playing Dungeons and Dragons or collecting footballers' autographs. Instead of keeping their passions to leisure times, how much more rewarding, educationally, if such out-of-school passions inspire inter-curricular links, helping them to learn with goodwill the 'boring bits' also, by amplifying personal aptitudes in a practical way. But in the present control system of mechanistic tick-boxes, this holistic approach is highly unlikely.

Yet in our most formative early years, we need to experience for ourselves more directly, and explore in a variety of ways, what the physicists now tell us; namely like the food chain, that all life is interconnected - and with all the elements. Like, for example, soil, soul and societies; caterpillars, butterflies and hurricanes. Also like oil, water, oxygen, blood, bones, proteins and Winnie the Pooh!

For ten years I taught philosophy to 4+-year-olds. In so doing, I discovered so much. With their help, I came to appreciate how the need to define oneself is always better served when lessons are person-centred rather than system-centred. Every metabolism, being unique like every mind, has individual requirements. If ignored, these can lead in later years to under achievement and illness. Ask the 100,000 students daily absent from school.

The child in us all loves to be playful. Given enough freedom, kids become absorbed in the moment, playing as they please. Watch them. Youngsters drop a toy (or a subject by daydreaming) the second it no longer nourishes them. In situations of coercion, no matter how subtle, you can see pupils close down. Aware students admire authentic enthusiasm but also see when bored teachers are on autopilot. Yet today, children are dragooned into schools, often enduring rather than enjoying the 'dog-training' exercises of imposed timetables. Worse, all forms of compulsion can generate resentment, anger and aggression - witness the second headline above, 'INCREASE IN PLAYGROUND BULLYING'

A sense of one's life's purpose supported, ideally, by a happy family environment, is essential for success. 'An unexamined life is not worth living' said Socrates. Through self-awareness, in any learner-teacher-learner situation, it is good for all to offer their own questions, seek their own answers. This approach cannot thrive in an atmosphere of fear While I was running a series of lessons on shapes and sizes, parents were able to watch on CD their offspring relish making choices rather than repeatedly looking over their shoulders to see if they were 'doing it right, sir'. To help this benign climate, apply this personalised reality check: For me, is it true, *is it necessary, is it kind?*

The real subject of any lesson for every special person is ME. So says every child until s/he is socialised, told not to be selfish but to conform. Bullying, like peer pressure, starts here. With home schooling becoming so popular, more people are rejecting the more common forms of state-imposed educational diet. It is only a legal requirement in this country to become educated, not to attend any registered school, even part-time. Facilitating the deepest aspirations found in the human condition as consciousness expands, no power on earth beats the creative joys of personal freedom. No wonder, so many state teachers seek early retirement!

A Complementary Learning Menu

So here is my plea for a deeper approach to personalised study, It would be offered, not imposed because I see the best of learning opportunities as an open-hearted invitation to learning, not as a hard-headed imperative.

Any teacher or tyrant who forces a student to learn will find that the indigestible educational fodder will get forgotten just as soon as the expedient of suitable grades have been achieved. Lack of kindness and respect can be killing to all sorts of personal initiatives. The word that Miliband's 'think-tank' for head teachers, staff and students chose to kick-start all 5 components of personalised learning was MUST.

So, alongside the slow-changing state system, my Learning Menu is offered as a *complementary* approach to whole-person learning, health and happiness. Over the years, many of us have been working almost under cover trying to re-invent education, just as certain medical practitioners have been pioneering complementary approaches to whole-person health and healing. So I am encouraging extra-curricula explorations into deeper self-examination, rather than letting so-called experts regulate our lives and, if we allow it, stunt our self-esteem. True balance knows that the two lobes of the human brain, the more literal left side and the more lateral right side, both need different ways of learning to enjoy life in all its variety of lessons.

What I am offering here is system in which each person is invited to contribute through negotiated activities, as if cooking one's own creative a la carte curriculum, in part alfresco, for the growing of organic fruit and vegetables for later cooking and consumption. Of all life skills, learning how to sustain optimum health and happiness is perhaps the highest. And that is not by eating processed, pre-packaged pellets of knowledge, like consuming chips with everything. It is never too early to start designing one's own curricula vitae. I have seen little ones become amazingly self-aware when suitably encouraged.

Body of Knowledge

Educationally, the most important examination could be the child's medical. What a scientific miracle is any one body. From molecules to muscles, from maths to magic, it contains every subject in the universe. How amazing are healthy hearts, brains, bones, blood, hair, nails, skin hands and feet. How educational is inner space as seen in x-rays, kirlian photography, endoscopy, cat-scans, infra-red technology, all extended perhaps, into computer games giving revealing 'Biofeedback'.

We are what we eat, so let's make a meal of it. Scientific research will produce personal proof of Jamie Oliver's claims about the detrimental effects of junk food in schools as in hospitals. It is not only wholesome food for the mind that makes a person feel well-nourished and glad to be alive – wholesome food for the body is just as important

Since all subjects are, inwardly, about ourselves first, they are ideally *subjective* in nature. The idea of persuading a student that all learning is *objective* is to risk that student turning into an object. And to extend the use of word play, the quicker he or she can object to this the better - an ideal approach to self-managed health and happiness.

Living on purpose - or learning in a spiritual vacuum? What I propose, as with extra-curricular classes I used to run within schools, is that we encourage a more creative, self-centred profile approach to learning. For all ages, that is truly the real Higher Education. For vital learners, an unexamined life is not worth living. Such **complementary** learning groups put direct experiences before second-hand explanations; people before paper; insightful management of all energy systems a shared priority throughout the Learning Centre and its supportive community. We all grow best by learning to make our own choices and live with the consequences.

Inwardly happy and healthy students do not need to experience bullying, drugs, junk food or designer clothes, let alone school uniforms. Self-satisfaction can become sufficient. A happy childhood lasts a lifetime, happiness a basic form of self-protection. Loved teenagers, secure in their own identity, need not become victims, get pregnant or catch venereal diseases. For us all, the real university is the universe, not as a collection of objects, but more like a communion of subjects. And in each case, the real subject in any learning centre is the self.

Through observation on all levels, the blueprint for each soul can be sensitively discerned. Complementary experiences would be encouraged in the arts and sciences of, say, meditation, healing, feng shui, yoga, martial arts, visualisation and by keeping dream journals. Profiles will be assembled to record and illustrate the development of personal achievements, together with goal-setting and goal-scoring. Students can be encouraged to set and assess their own forms of self-examination. Keeping faith in their common sense can also be seen as spiritual.

Some Faith Schools are already using gifted students as 'Lead Learners' to help their peers in class. So far, this is only in the realm of academic enterprises, not yet extended into organic gardening, cooking, plumbing and electrical engineering. The current government, while championing enquiry-based independent learning schemes of work, still insists that every differentiated child MUST wear a school uniform

By loving all peoples, by learning one's unique mission on earth by way of giving service, this is the central ache that, ignored, nags the unenlightened. When a soul is not just on message but on mission, all the boring chores we all have to tackle can be accommodated without angst or anger, rage or resentment; indeed, without the need, countrywide, for 400 government-imposed 'sin-bins'. In a civilised learning society, the only 'sin' is unhealthy, unappetising unhappiness.

With a Complementary Learning Menu, devoted to personalised faith, hope and charity, such unhappiness becomes less likely.

Christopher Gilmore has taught all ages, in four continents, a range of self-development skills. His many pioneering 'Playshops' include, Star Children; Creative Philosophy; Active Storytelling & Soul-Centred Education, the title of his latest book. As an actor he produces his own Talking Books, like Bright Eyes and Bubbles. As a teacher he writes DOVETALES, 10 guidebooks to stimulate Creativity Across the Curriculum. As a novelist he offers ALICE IN WELFARELAND. His unpublished book, ANGEL EDUCATION, contains a full version of The Learning Menu outlined in the chapter above.

www.christophergilmore.com
Email: chrisgilmore.souled@virgin.net

EDUCATION FOR ECOLOGICAL VIABILITY THROUGH CO-OPERATIVE ACTION

Gary McIntyre Boyd.

"No man is an island, entire of itself...every man is part of the main....I am involved in mankind; and therefore, never send to know for whom the bell tolls; it tolls for thee"
John Donne.

This chapter deals with five important questions:

1. What is education for?

2. Why must education be re-invented now?

3. What sort of re-invented education should we envision?

4. How to carry out such education?

5. How can we persuade people to implement and adopt our educational innovations?

1. What is education for?

Education, broadly defined, is our main way to develop and live as better humans. Lifelong, mutual education is perhaps the highest human end, not just a means for economic prosperity or cultural reproduction. The purpose of human life is arguably to learn and perform ever more wonderful and delightful ways of being in the world together. Education is essential to the "modern vocabulary of hope that depends on progress; on the belief that what makes lives worth living is that they can be improved" (Appignanesi, 2005). Education happens everywhere people teach and learn.

Institutionalised education was invented to help to tame or civilise youth and to pass on the heritage of skills, knowledge, attitudes and commitments of each community to succeeding

213

generations. Since the time of the "gymnasia" of Athens and Sparta, it has been used to train and select youth for specialised roles in society. Finally in all urban societies, schools have served the important function of keeping the young, who cannot be immediately employed, out of the way of others. "The devil finds work for idle hands!" Organised schooling increases the influence of the peer group which in turn has exerted a major educative, or often dis-educative, influence, that limits the effectiveness of the schools.

In the nineteenth century, universal primary schooling was invented and implemented in Europe and the USA., to train workers for industry and commerce. In the first half of the twentieth century, universal secondary schooling was invented and post-secondary education was deployed to meet the more complex needs of business and government. In the second half of the twentieth century, the mass media were perfected to sell ever more goods and services through "advertainment". Inadvertently they became a dominant educational (and mis-educational) influence competing with schools, families and churches everywhere. Now in the 21st century the Internet and portable interactive entertainment devices, again introduced as business ventures, are assuming a major educative (and dis-educative) role almost everywhere on Earth. So we can see that education has already been re-invented many times, and continues to be re-invented in major ways.,

2. Why must we reinvent education now?

The too short answer is: for decent human survival. We must again re-invent education now to teach people strategies and technologies which really can produce plausible hope of improving world civilisation so that it won't continue to commit suicide.

Without massive and deep re-education by the mid twenty-first century, more and more people everywhere will be doomed to nasty, brutal and short lives (Heilbroner, 1974, Wright, 2004, Diamond 2004). If business and politics go on as usual, billions of people will suffer miserably from the global consequences of our, and their, competitive consumption. Climate change and violent weather, pandemic disease, water and air pollution, depletion of non-renewable resources, and probably much ideological and religious terrorism, if not large WMD wars, will result. So, if we do not somehow vastly improve human beings and human institutions through education, it is now clear to those of us who do not assiduously avert our eyes, that anything we would care to call desirable human life is unlikely to prevail to the end of this century.

At the beginning of the twentieth century, H. G. Wells said, "history is a race between education and disaster." Depending on where and when you looked, both could be said to win in the twentieth century. Now, in the twenty-first century, history continues to be a race between education and disaster, but we are all, all around the world, coupled so much more closely together that both cannot win.

The Earth's available resources are strictly limited by the kinds and amounts of pollution we will tolerate (Reid, 2005). Nuclear energy can be abundant but at the cost of very long-lasting radioactive pollution and much waste heat. Fossil fuels produce greenhouse gases which contribute to global warming, climate change and destructive storms. Coal energy will be abundant for this century but with very high immediate pollution costs. Gas and oil supplies are increasingly being exhausted. In any case, more energy use means more global warming, and more extinction of fish, animals and plants. Within ten years serious climate change will be irreversible (Exeter, 2005).

The Earth's human population is now expected to peak at about nine billion at around 2040. This means that at least one third more persons than we have now will be competing for dwindling resources and competing to avoid pollution. The competition between the have-nots and the haves is unlikely to be peaceful. China buys almost all of Canada's coal. There could perhaps be war between China and the USA over the Alberta Tar-sands vast oil reserves.

At present about one third of the Earth's population - over

two billion people - are nowhere near a condition of peace and well being. For instance, according to UNESCO, a child dies of malnutrition roughly every four seconds! As for the prospects for universal lasting peace and well being, notwithstanding our marvellous scientific advances, these seem to be getting poorer day by day. One response to seeing and hearing all this, is despair. More and more young people exposed to the world via mass media, and denied meaningful work, are committing suicide.

A slightly longer answer is: because we now understand the nature of human learning in radically different ways. Mind is in bodies and it runs across bodies and computers and communications machines. Mind-body dualism is now thoroughly discredited, and consequently so-called `physical education' and mental education now are seen to be better undertaken in activities which involve both at once. The old individual-society dualism is also no longer tenable - see the work of Vygotsky and Bhaktin (Morson, 1981) in the early 20th century, and the more recent work by Pask, Resnick, Gergen.

Fortunately now we have the metaphor of the "distributed computer program" to draw upon. An example is the SETTI program: thousands of people have loaded parts of this onto their own PCs and left it to run online with the other parts all over the world, whenever they are not using their PC for something else. Another example is the World Wide Web. taken as a whole, this is one immense computing system distributed over millions of people's computers.

Major religions are similar: each member of the faithful has part of the program and it is executed when they perform the rituals etc. of the religion. Groups, who function together to act publicly on a large scale, have behaviour patterns which are incorporated in the nervous systems of the group.

So education needs to be reinvented to educate these distributed programs/networks, not just individuals. This emphasis on educating collectives is not to depreciate the sacredness or preciousness of each unique individual, whatever her or his condition or capabilities may be. Quite the contrary, it is necessary to educate networks to prevent people being pressured by groups or institutions to maltreat other people. The failure to treat any human being, as a fellow human being, whose basic hopes and fears are respected, is evil.

We urgently need to shift from education for competitive business and political success to education for long-term co-operation for ecological viability. The narcissistic attitudes, short-term focused attention and ruthless competitive skills required to succeed in business and politics effectively ensure that the people and organisations which acquire most power are seriously unfit to make the decisions and take the actions required for long-term human survival. It is only rarely that a humanitarian such as Bill Gates gets to the top of business, or that a wise man such as George Soros sees humanitarian light after gaming his way to the top of the global financial casino.

Occasionally a statesman, a Roosevelt, an Eisenhower, or a Trudeau, gains great political power while retaining an intelligent and farsighted understanding of the human predicament. But mostly our hyper-successful businessmen and politicians are extremely myopic. They make use of opportunistic trader tricks to buy temporary allies who will support their current gambits (Jacobs, Jane, 1992). A better education must inculcate humanitarian guardian values, creativity values, deep respect for science, deep scepticism of competitive games and generally long-term global perspectives. Unfortunately, such people tend to get blown out of the way by the organised competitive gamesters. The four richest men in the world have more personal wealth than over two billion poor in the forty-odd poorest countries.

Consequently a better education must help far-sighted, ecologically responsible people to learn how to outsmart and out-compete the selfish gamesters, without losing sight of long term humanitarian and ecological sustainability goals. Since a smart individual totally specialised for winning will beat another smart individual whose attention is divided between winning and virtue, success can be possible only through the education not of merely individuals but also, and especially, of groups and networks. Teams beat loners. Networks, teams and some organisations of responsible citizens (e.g. the Sierra Club, Amnesty International, Mèdicins sans Frontieres and Greenpeace) have shown real ability to outmanoeuvre huge competitive institutions.

3. What sort of reinvented education should we envision?

What might an ideal vision be, and then what exactly is possible, in the way of world-wide, life-long learning that will promote viability? Only openly accessible worldwide life-long education offers any realistic prospects for lasting improvements in global peace and happiness. We must help re-invent education for all so that: -

- we will breed less
- we will all learn to live symbiotically with the Earth's eco-systems
- we will learn to live harmoniously with each other's cultures and religions.

This may seem impossible, but the cost of not trying is despair and certain failure. Five factors are essential –
Creative imagination
Scientific understanding
Technical capability
Political legitimacy
Far-sighted love

What should be learned? Better curricula are needed from childhood onward to develop a holistic and principled understanding of the behaviour of complex coupled systems which are adaptive and proactive. Conventional subject specialisation in education obscures the real connectivity which is occurring everywhere and all the time. The artificial boundaries between the sciences the humanities and the arts need to be bridged. We need to engage in learning conversations about the ethical, moral and aesthetic aspects of nature and of human works throughout our lives.

For viability, education should be as much the education of communities and networks, as the education of individual persons. Education is not a product or a service; it is a transformative process where collective selves as well as individual selves are involved. Education is certainly not just an individual consumer good; it necessarily always implicates others. It is true that skills training can be individual and even machine 'delivered', but that is not education - although it is at times a pre-requisite for education. The development of attitudes, appropriate feelings, commitments and deep understanding, and especially the development of wise decision-making capabilities together, are intrinsically social undertakings.

It is beneficial to think in terms of educating three sorts of human actors: - sub-personalities (or personae), individuals and networks/organisations. Sub-personalities are our particular collection of personae which act out in certain classes of situations. What the child learns at home continues to be exhibited in home-type family roles for the rest of their life, but less often acts out in work or public or military roles (and vice-versa).

Organisational actors, such as teams, religious communities, some businesses, etc. involve many persons, who carry important parts of the 'programme' for the organisation. The organisation enlists them in coherent performances, where they semi-automatically execute their parts of the programme together, thus socially constructing their world. Organisations can learn, without the individual member being necessarily aware of it; they can have intentions and act coherently.

The effective 'God" of any particular religious society is such a distributed programme across members, one which is often imagined by them to be consciously intentional. Most God religions are now badly in need of re-education since they were developed in pastoral or primitive farming societies, when people had very little real power over anything except each other and their animals. Now, that situation has been totally superseded through the development of technology which

219

can, and quite possibly will, destroy, all human life on Earth. Consequently our God(s) are in need of re-educating to take these new powers into account. If education is re-invented for survival, peace and happiness, it must be particularly designed to undertake a continuing process of re-educating the 'Gods' of all major religions!

4. How to carry out such education?

This would be achieved through team game simulations, ones that are dramatically involving, and have associated subsequent learning conversations. These would be conducted, first of all in the safety of cyberspace". The most potent educational activities we have are face-to-face dramatic role-play activities (Schutzman & Chen-Cruz, 1994). The activities with most worldwide outreach are on-line games (Alexander, 2003). The challenge for educational technologists today, is to combine these into high quality openly accessible learning support systems.

It is generally understood (though not by the 40% of Americans, who, according to Gallup, do not believe in evolution) that life emerged from non-living matter hundreds of million years ago and that homo-sapiens sapiens emerged from other primate life about forty million years ago, all through variation and natural selection. Contemporary systems science recognises many levels of emergent systemic complexity. Simple rules of chemistry led to the emergence of organic molecules, physical laws and chance events led those to combine into living cells once on this planet, and that was enough to start the emergence of multitudinous life forms.

The levels of complex adaptive systems which I believe are most important to be identified and used for reinventing education, are listed below in their historical evolutionary order of increasing complexity. They are: -
1) trivial automata,
2) subsisting systems,
3) self-reproducing systems,
4) viral parasitic systems,

5) negotiating systems,
6) competitive linguistic-identity elaborating and propagating systems,
7) emancipative systems (from bad habits and addictions),
8) math-science-philosophy re-creative   elaborating   and correcting systems. (Boyd, 2000)

These eight levels of emergent systems must be well understood if people are to be able to co-steer the world wisely. Therefore, we must repeatedly carry out assessments of learner's growing ability to recognise, acquire and deploy requisite control variety at each of the complex adaptive systems levels.

5. How can we persuade people to implement and adopt our educational innovations?

Potent educational activities transform people to some extent and therefore must be legitimated. The politics of curriculum and assessment are well known. The micro-politics determining the ethicality of activities or treatments among teachers, students and researchers also has a large literature. For the most part, our traditionally legitimate schooling activities have not been very potent at transforming people. However newer technologies starting with radio, films and television and going on to massive virtual reality gaming have increasingly become more potent people changers.

Entertainment technologies and educational technology are beginning to be really potent people changers. Soon their practitioners will need to be as carefully trained, licensed and monitored as engineers or surgeons. In general, as Habermas (1973-1975) pointed out, there are three bases other than brute force or seduction, for legitimating practice: 1) The historical: - we have always done it this way so it is OK, or "that's what I learned in school so that's what my kids should learn". 2) The expert-scientific:, e.g. studies on class size show that learning achievement improves greatly for class sizes below fifteen pupils, getting better the smaller the group; therefore we should have quite small classes in schools. 3) The representative stakeholder, e.g. "I listen and speak for the other parents, he listens and speaks for the local tax-payers, she listens and speaks for the children in her kindergarten, he attends to and speaks for the nation of those buried and those yet unborn". Whatever re-invention of education we undertake should involve non-dominative networking as an intrinsic functional component, if it is to be implanted and thrive around the world.

Necessary Technology for non-dominative political discourse

Democracy that is truly participatory requires some means for all stakeholders to engage in free and fair discussion about what should be done and with which priorities. This is clearly not possible face-to-face except in times and places of exceptional good will. I suggest that communications mediated by new communication technologies can enable everyone with a mobile phone who wishes to do so to put their arguments and desires into political play. The "bloggosphere" already allows anyone to publish arguments and opinions linked to any other Web documents. These and other types of Internet communications are already having appreciable political effects (such as the Dean campaign in the U.S.). However, as yet, there is no way directly to link such soundings to the decision-making, action and enforcement being carried out in either corporations or governments. State of the art information technology is however, almost good enough to provide such truly democratic steering systems now.

Conclusion

I conclude that it would be very difficult, almost impossible, to achieve but still very much worth trying. How can such an approach hope to compete against the normative imperatives of massive institutions (Max Weber) and the ubiquitous short-sightedness born of fear (Becker, 1975) or greed? At this juncture, I think that the best educational re-invention programme that can now be offered is the systemic development of drama and simulations. These would be , supported by IT as well as satellite broadcasting and would be embedded in learning conversations designed to generate understanding of the complex systems we are in.

Dr. Gary McIntyre Boyd is Professor of Education, Liaison Director Educational Technology Doctoral Programme, and co-director with Dr. Vladimir Zeman of the Centre for System Research and Knowledge Engineering at Concordia University, Montreal Canada. also Associate Director Academic Liaison AudioVisual Dept.

His main interest is Educational/Cultural Cybernetics and he has published a dozen descriptive and prescriptive papers on the subject in Journals such as the British Journal of Educational Technology, the Association for Educational and Training Technology Journal and the Canadian Journal for Educational Communications

References

a complete list of References is available from the author boyd@education.concordia.ca or from the SEI website, www.excite-education.org

REFOUNDING EDUCATION ON EVOLUTIONARY PSYCHOLOGY

Mike Doyle

Setting the scene

Beryl sat at the middle of the class watching Mr Chipps explain addition. Standing, replete with headset in front of the whiteboard, the sums he gave the class appeared, as if by magic, on the board as he spoke. All the class needed to do was shout out the answer. Unfortunately for our teacher, Denis, Beryl's older brother, having been excluded permanently for trying to reprogram the one-arm-bandits in the town's arcade, had hacked into the system and re-programmed the whiteboard.

The webcam used to watch the children from the back of the room was now programmed to detect the direction of gaze of the teacher. So, when he was not looking, the whiteboard evaluated the sum and displayed the answer on the screen. More happened when no teacher was present. Watching the whiteboard doing its own sums, Beryl wondered for a moment why Mr Chipps thought it so important for her to learn things the machine could do so much better, but remembering that these were the basic skills she was tested on she put the dreamy little thought away and got on with her real work.

Introduction

The psychology that underpins education is the standard social science model (Cosmides and Tooby 1), the psychology outlined in introductory psychology texts written for 'A' level students and undergraduate courses. It informs much educational research. Our evolution is not considered, nor is our ability to draw. Conversely perception, language, and personality have chapters devoted to them. This omission is fascinating because we are what we evolved to be and our whole technological creation is dependent upon our capacity to draw out ideas.

Philosophers and linguists alike seem not to notice technology and maintain that language is our most awesome, crowning achievement. Education privileges this standpoint, with English taking pride of place at the head of the English National Curriculum. (The same is true of other cultures). I seek to challenge this assumption and to develop an approach to education that respects our actual evolved capabilities. I aim to dig a foundation trench for an education matched to our peculiar evolved adaptations. I am aware that the notion of evolution is not universally supported. I use this extremely useful theory in my work, and commend it.

The evolutionary context

An alternative to the standard social science model is evolutionary psychology (2). Unfortunately, this field peters out when it reaches the final chapter, usually entitled "Culture." The question of how we do a drawing remains unaddressed. To lift the fog we need to dig into palaeontology and the evolution of genus Homo, to which our species belongs (3). I will sketch sufficient of this to establish my position. For those who wish to delve further I provide a short bibliography. However, I must caution that this is a field not without controversy and the trajectory I trace differs from that, for instance, currently displayed in a case at Manchester Museum.

We trace the evolution of our species from a split with the great apes some five million years ago. A coarse-grained, somewhat out-dated, analysis would progress as follows:
   from Homo habilis (c.2.5Million years ago)
   through Homo erectus (c.1.8Million years ago)
   and archaic Homo sapiens (c.500 thousand years ago)
   to us, H sapiens sapiens (c.150 thousand years)
There is little argument that what might be called culture and creativity appeared at the same time as we did, or even later. The same cannot be said for language.

Language evolution

There are certain physiological features necessary for speech of human complexity. Three characteristics traced in the fossil record are: Broca's and Wernike's areas in the brain (from skull endocasts); the descent of the larynx to provide the voice box (from flexion of the basicranium); and greater enervation of the chest and tongue to give more control over breathing and articulation (from spinal nerve passage size). It appears that as the brain gets bigger, so these three features become more prominent. All members of the genus Homo had speech of some sort. Homo erectus had a larynx which could have been about where it is in an eight-year-old child. The Neanderthals may well have had a modern speech system. Our more direct precursors, anatomically modern H sapiens, certainly did. So, why did speech evolve, given that there is a great risk of choking from a descended larynx?

The social brain hypothesis of evolutionary psychology – an explanation of our successful co-operation with strangers – provides a clue. Dunbar (4) suggests that speech developed from primate grooming, the cement of simple alliances, to provide a facilitative mechanism for species reciprocal altruism.

Reciprocal altruism is a genetically risky strategy. It benefits the selfish gene (5) only if co-operation can be assured; because defection (freeriding) is the best strategy if you don't get caught. Reciprocal altruism has three prerequisites: memory for people and events; individuals who can recognise one another; and 'tit-for-tat' as the rule of the game. Under these conditions an evolutionary stable state, a balance of co-operators and freeriders is established. (Freeriders, are not driven to extinction because tit-for-tat requires individuals to co-operate on first meeting). This sets up an evolutionary arms race between co-operators and freeriders. The fruits of this are seen in the complexity of sound and grammar in human language. The sound system is so finely tuned that accent can change within 25 kilometres – a stranger is more likely to be a freerider than a local. Similarly, grammar allows subject, object and verb to swap places.

These two effects allow mutually incomprehensible languages easily to develop – a means of generating group cohesion (6). Of these characteristics of human language, accent certainly, and grammar probably, were present in species prior to us. I suspect that the capacity that underpins the way we coin new words existed in pre-human languages. So, language developed before us.

Technicity

First, let me deal with tools. Although stone tools developed in sophistication across the species Homo habilis, erectus, and archaic sapiens including the Neanderthals, within each species the toolkit remained virtually unchanged throughout its existence - over a million years for Homo erectus. At the earliest (7), signs of anything approaching modern technology is found some 250,000 years ago but then intermittently in the record until after we arrived. So, stone tools per se do not categorise us, although I hope to show that technology does.

The toolkits of all species prior to ours were highly conservative. We may contrast the million years of stability of Homo erctus with the 150,000 year trajectory from a standing start to genetic engineering for us. This suggests a different basis for tool making in the two species. There are two possible genetic bases for tool making. The most common is what Dawkins (8) calls the 'extended phenotype,' which may be characterised by birds' nests and conceptualised as firmware in the computing sense. The alternative is culturally learned behaviour. A non-human example of this is found in chimpanzee troupes. Termite fishing is peculiar to specific troupes and the stick-tools used of different design. Knowledge is passed down generations but can be lost.

I use 'technicity' to denote this learned, tool making culture. The word originates in the philosophy of Martin Heidegger (9), whose formulation I reconstruct as, *the capability of behaviourally modern humans to dominate the earth by controlling beings that are considered as objects,* thereby shifting technicity's emergence from the post-Socratic Greeks to our emergence as a species. Whilst the neurological mechanism of technicity is unknown, technicity is evidenced by our capacity to draw, to combine point, line, and arc, and create novel images; by our capacity to combine ingredients and processes to cook meals, ferment wine, blend perfume, and isolate scents; and by our capacity to analyse sound and create wind and string instruments to make music.

All languages are equally complex and expressive and the only progress made by our species has been through technology and its mathematical offspring, science. This demonstrates, for me, the intellectual dominance of technicity over language

Technicity is a highly risky evolutionary strategy with only culture as a mode of transmission. It can be viable only in a population of reciprocal co-operators, which is a prerequisite. It follows, therefore, that language is a necessary precursor for the evolution of technicity, but not sufficient. The role of language is in 'making the bargain' not in creating the goods. The general communication system of technicity is drawing. The blueprint, exploded diagram, flat-pack assembly instruction, LEGO-style instruction sequence, and so on, are far more universally comprehensible than would be the same when expressed in a particular human language, albeit in writing.

External memory

Writing, upon which our education system is founded, illustrates the major adaptive advantage of technicity: external memory. All species prior to us were constrained in their development by what they could keep, and do, in their heads. The uncreative Neanderthals actually had bigger brains than us. By getting memory and mechanism out of our heads and into the environment, we opened up the possibility of progress. *Education is about maximising the benefits of this, our unique, awesome adaptation.*

Education

We confuse ourselves mightily when we talk education. Language develops instinct-like (10) in early childhood and needs no formal teaching. All species bring up their offspring. Education is required only because of our unique burden of technicity. Every child needs to be taught how to use, make, and develop tools of trades. From the bread oven to the silicon chip furnace our skills and knowledge are maintained and advanced through education. So powerful is the adaptation of external memory that we not only maintain our level of knowledge but increment it generation on generation, if conditions are favourable (11). In today's energy-rich and information-rich circumstances, universal text-based education, which fits individuals to perform highly differentiated roles in a hyper-co-operative society, has proved particularly effective.

The problem that we face stems from the very information-richness that texts have generated. Literacy is the foundation stone of school. Literacy is writing. Writing is an external memory technology. And yet the focus of teaching is on the 'story' and the enjoyment of reading, with a presumption that an appreciation of literature is the prime objective. To this end, style, spelling, and script are the focus - the exigencies of the craft-making technology a fetish and dragging technicity down an evolutionary step. This trajectory in the universal education systems originating in the nineteenth century was an inevitable consequence of the combined effects of the evolutionary necessity of language and the communication requirements of developing industry.

The development of the stored program digital computer, in the late 1940s, has totally changed the character of our external memory system. Text can only store data. All operations must be carried out either in the head or with a dedicated machine. Thus, in writing English, the pen and the paper make up the machine with all the rest hanging upon learning. Digital machines carry out programmed operations on data, i.e. what we do in the head. Today they can convert speech directly into writing and back again. This they can do for children from the age of seven upwards: the age at which many European cultures begin to teach reading and writing. A question arises For what purpose do we require children to be literate?

Literacy binds speech and technicity together. (Note that I do not use the word language here.) It grabs fugitive speech out of thin air and entombs it on the page. Once frozen it is open to inspection, to modification, to thought. It becomes accessible to objective study. Literacy is the means technicity uses fully to co-opt speech to its intellectual ends. Our human intellect lies not in speech but in the mental processes that underpin technicity. Co-option of speech is required only for diffusion of the concepts technicity creates.

Primate matters

Institutions and the structure and smooth functioning of our society (including school itself) are dependent upon more than technicity, although it is their origin. The behaviours and developmental characteristics inherited from our primate precursors are the underlying context (12). So, any education system devised for the twenty-first century needs to acknowledge our knowledge in this domain. This will offer a radical perspective upon the moral, ethical, interpersonal, sex and civic aspects of the school curriculum. To date these aspects have been informed by religious, philosophical, and political thought.

It is time to stand aside from their verbal formulations and look our evolutionary history in the face. Much of the behaviour that we seek to suppress is rooted in pre-human primate patterns of behaviour; many of the socially constructive behaviours we now value have their genesis within no longer extant species Homo as, facilitated by speech, hyper-co-operation evolved. And much that is moral and ethical is rooted in the freerider/ co-operator conflict and control, and its genetic correlates.

Curriculum matters

The curriculum of today's schools has developed under the social pressures of the times and epochs that led to the present. Its beginnings are to be found in the scribal schools on Sumer some six millennia ago. Greek and Roman concepts were built on by Judeo-Christian formulations; most notably, the Carolingian. Renaissance thinking combined a Classical regression with Islamic science and Hindu-Arabic mathematics. By the middle of the nineteenth century, universal elementary education founded in literacy, numeracy, and some science and technology, was developing as the separate streams of academe and trade came together in industrialised repetition production.

By the beginning of the twentieth century the fundamentals of today's subject-based curriculum had been established. Today's hierarchy (English, Mathematics, Science, Design and Technology, ICT, History, Geography, Modern Foreign Language, Art and Design, Music, Physical Education, and Citizenship, plus PHSE) is probably more utilitarian than previously, with the arts losing ground. Emphasis on standards of attainment gave rise to (text-focused) National Literacy and Numeracy Strategies, constraining ICT to "the ability to use a wider range of information sources ..." This placed ICT in a different, distanced, conceptual category from literacy and numeracy.

The relationship of ICT to literacy and numeracy, the Victorian 3Rs, is of particular interest. Recall, the latter originated in Sumer for administrative recording. Since then, the trajectory of numerical notation has taken us into the realm of the algorithm and computing. The trajectory of writing, has taken us into the two cultures: technical and literary. Literature is interesting because the various systems of writing that have been developed are very poor for recording much of speech. Indeed, little beyond syntax and morphology is frozen on the page. One of the great secrets children need to learn is that most of speech is not noted: the skill of the literary writer is in implying what is not there. Text-to-speech synthesisers show

how skeletal a representation of speech writing is. Speech recognition systems work in reverse, stripping out all the music of speech to extract the underlying lexicon and syntax.

Technical language is different: it is not intended to be spoken and originates within writing; thus, it is possible for Stephen Hawking to lecture using text-to-speech. Embedded in both Literacy and Numeracy strategies lies the assertion that literacy and numeracy skills are necessarily taught by oral/ mental methods. The prescribed progression: oral – textual – computational, is asserted to be natural. Certainly it follows the evolutionary sequence; but is it really necessary for young children to emulate Neanderthals and do everything in their head?

I suggest that digital media could let children into the secret of the notation, which knowledge they could then apply to unlocking the complex relation it has with reality. This would entail change in teaching methods of a scale unknown in education history. Timing such a change in relation to the maturity of ICT will be a very delicate matter.

The same is true for the curriculum itself. The evolutionary perspective offers a major revision of education. But how does nationalistic history metamorphose into the study of our species? How do we move from doings of 'leaders' to the unrecorded progress of technicity? How do we shift from a mother/other tongue view of language to its nature as an adaptation? How do we privilege technology equally with science; and where do we place mathematics?

Education has always had two faces: preparation for living and celebration of our humanity. Philosophers' assertions notwithstanding, our crowning cognitive capability is not language: it is technicity. Education heretofore has concurred with the philosophers. Real restructuring requires a vigorous challenge to this basic presumption, coupled with a willingness to look ourselves in the face.

Reinventing education

ICT will slowly bring about a dawning realisation that the 'basics', which alienate many children, are not basic at all. Spelling and sums will become games and handwriting a part of art. When we come to terms with technology, teaching becomes more than ever a social exercise The classroom becomes a window on the world. No longer are teachers passing on their own craft skills and knowledge. Subjects are slices though the British Library database instead of isolated texts.

Our species conflates two adaptations: language, which communicates through speech and is highly interpersonal; and technicity, which communicates through graphics and gadgets and enables objectivity. The problem for education is that technicity co-opts language, largely by modifying and extending the vocabulary. This means that much that might be remarked goes unremarked, so remains unacknowledged. We need to unravel this intimate relationship. It is not a task for language: clarity comes through science founded on evolution rather than philosophy rooted in language. Progress demands a developmental approach to restructuring education: research and development leading to reformulation as we realise that perception tricks us and the earth actually goes round the sun. The shift from text to digital media may catalyse the step-change.

Mike Doyle taught for a quarter of a century, was involved in educational technology, including chairing the British Logo User Group, before ICT and whiteboards became fashionable. He always wondered why certain things computers could do well were taboo in school. A member of BERA, he is the occupant of www.logios.org

References

1. Barkow J H, Cosmides L & Tooby J eds 1992
    The Adapted Mind Oxford: Oxford University Press
2. Barrett L Dunbar R & Lycett J 2002 *Human Evolutionary*

Psychology Basingstoke: Palgrave
3. Lewin R 1998 Principles of *Human Evolution* Malden Mass: Blackwell Scientific
4. Dunbar R 2004 *Grooming Gossip and the Evolution of Language* London: Faber and Faber
5. Dawkins R 1989 *The Selfish Gene* Oxford: Oxford University Press
6. Nettle D 1999 *Linguistic Diversity* New York: Oxford University Press
7. McBrearty S and Brooks AS 2000 The Revolution that Wasn't *Journal of Human Evolution* 39 5 453-563
8. Dawkins R 1999 *The Extended Phenotype* Oxford: Oxford University Press
9. Krell DF *Basic Writings* London: Routledge
10. Pinker S 1994 *The Language Instinct* London: Allen Lane The Penguin Press
11. Diamond J 1998 *Guns, Germs and Steel* London: Jonathan Cape
12. Goodall J 1986 *The Chimpanzees of the Gombe* London: Belknap Press of the University of Harvard

A GRUMPY OLD PEDAGOGUE'S VIEWS OF EDUCATION.

Michael J. Hicks

Reinventing 'education', starting from scratch? That **is** a challenge! It is relatively easy to look at the existing system and list what we do not want: for example, a 'one system fits all' national curriculum that is far too prescriptive, homework, league tables that do not truly reflect the value added, a multi-tier university system, etc. It is not so easy to start with a blank piece of paper and say what we do want.

Initially, I was going to cheat and start with what should be scrapped before offering some ideas about doing things differently and then finishing with some new ideas. On reflection, I realized that most of the things I wanted to say fell into the category of 'doing things differently'; that is, there is very little I really wanted to 'disappear without a trace', and most of my 'new' ideas were far from new.

I am grateful to my wife and two of my friends, who, unlike me, still work in secondary schools, for some of the ideas/opinions expressed below.

There have been two main problems with education as it has developed over the decades. Firstly, when something has been seen to be deficient, there has been a tendency to rush in and introduce a new way of doing things without fully appreciating its implications and repercussions, rather than to stop and consider what was good (and worth keeping) about the old way. Next time we make some changes, let's not do this again.

Secondly, there has been too much political intervention, both from politicians seeking to please those who might (re)elect them, and from an overzealous politically correct 'movement'; to a lesser or greater extent, politics pervades most things

A Grumpy Old Pedagogue's Views of Education.

Forward to the Past!

There is a case, I believe, for revisiting some of the things we have thrown away in the past, in our haste to solve 'problems'. Some examples are:

1. Practical skills

The National Curriculum's Design & Technology (D&T) replaced subjects like technical drawing, woodwork, metal work, cooking, etc., some of which are valuable life skills, and all should be available both for those who want to do them and also for those who do not wish, or (dare I say it) those unsuited, to follow the academic route. The result is that there is very little training in these skills in schools. Let us bring some of it back into schools.

But do not repeat the mistake! Do not throw out the essence of D&T. Seeing how these practical skills fit into the bigger picture, including design, problem solving, implementation planning, costing, marketing, etc. should somehow be retained. We decry the fact that many (especially traditional) crafts are disappearing. What could be better than to enable someone with an interest and ability in one (or more) of them to develop the practical skills **and**, at the same time, the ability to make a living from them?

2. The sixth form curriculum

The idea of broadening the sixth form curriculum (five subjects instead of the more usual three) is not new. My master's dissertation literature review written in the early 70s cited several prior suggestions that never came to fruition. I have always been a firm believer in a broader sixth form education. Now at last we have done something - 4AS + 3A2. It was supposed to be 5AS, but that was deemed 'unworkable' - another less than perfect compromise. This is a classic example of building a prototype and putting it straight into service whilst at the same time testing it and sorting out its shortcomings. Let's have another go at it.

3. Multi-tier 'universities'

What drives the present desire to send 50 per cent of 18 year olds to university ? And to force them to go into substantial debt for the privilege? Certainly, unless there is a major rethink as to what a university is, and how it is funded, this is untenable.

Universities should certainly be more inclusive than they were when I attended in the late 60s, but I am not convinced that 50% of school leavers want and will benefit from the sort of university education I had (at what was then a new 'mostly concrete with some red bricks' university). We are all different and have different aspirations and capabilities, all of which are valuable. We should be providing a diverse higher education, instead of forcing the universities at the bottom of the pile to 'dumb down' their degrees to attract and keep students. What was so wrong with the old concept of a polytechnic?

The old polytechnics were certainly the equal of the many established universities, even though they tended to approach things (curriculum, research, etc.) in different ways – what we might crudely describe as an 'applied' rather than a 'pure' approach. Some of the newer ones were still 'true' polytechnics and served a different market requirement.

When the college of higher education I taught at became a part of the last of the 'new' polytechnics, I really felt proud. I could identify with the idea that we were filling the gap left by the old polytechnics that had now moved on to other things. We were formed from institutions that taught courses from craft catering and those for laboratory technicians, through nursing and music, to taught masters degrees and professional qualifications!

But then we were forced to become a university! We could never compete for funding (a large amount of which was based on our non-existent research profile - we were a teaching organization) or in any other way, with the older established universities, and why should we have had to? Now we have four tiers of university, (1) the 'old' universities e.g. Oxford, Cambridge, Durham, (2) the 'red brick' universities e.g. Manchester, Bristol, Birmingham, (3) the 'new' universities (and the ones in between) e.g. Sussex, Warwick, Leicester, a range of 'polytechnic' universities e.g. Bath, Portsmouth, de Montford, and (4) the 'even newer' universities e.g. Bournemouth, Thames Valley. Why not call them different things and allow them to service different market segments, in a different way, if that is appropriate?

4. Student Funding

The concept of student loans and tuition fees is ill founded and is putting off the very people we are trying to include in higher education. Realistic maintenance grants should be brought back for all but the more affluent families (say where combined incomes are twice the average wage, but this is negotiable) and should take into account the number of children per family in higher education at any one time. And if you must, introduce a graduate tax. However, most graduates (except some working in the public sector!) get a higher wage than non-graduates and therefore pay more tax anyway.

We should abolish tuition fees completely and fund higher education properly. A lot of money has gone into schools (not always in the right places), but despite saying how important higher education is, that sector has been seriously under-funded by successive governments. The state and its citizens benefit from a well-educated work force and should pay for it. But it would seem that you cannot raise taxes and get elected!

5. Ofsted

I propose we conduct some impartial research into whether the **actual** improvements in school performance Ofsted has achieved, is commensurate with the resentment in and stress caused to teachers.

Bring back the old system with HM Inspectors only. As young

teachers we went in fear and trepidation of their imminent arrival, but at least they were supportive, constructive in their criticism, and knew what they were talking about.

6. Apprenticeships

An encouraging trend in education is a tendency to revisit (though this is not always realized by the proposers!) past abandoned/ discredited concepts, such as the recent announcement to (re)invent what we used to call apprenticeships. Some of the old schemes were a good learning experience for the apprentice and very satisfying for the person imparting their knowledge and skills, while others were an abuse of one party or another. Everything depended on to whom you were apprenticed, but why did we allow this concept to disappear in the recession when firms could not afford training?

7. Local Management of Schools (LMS)

Abandon LMS and return to the days of LEA control. The school board of governors, volunteers who often know very little about the details of running a successful school, are now the employers and the ultimate arbiters of the efficiency/ performance of their school and its strategy (or lack of it). Since the introduction of LMS, teachers have been made redundant rather than redeployed, LEA's no longer have the funds to provide all the support services they used to offer, and have lost much of their ability to plan strategic development of education on a community wide basis.

Things that must change

1. The National Curriculum

Children and students are not all the same and so a national curriculum of the type we have now, which seems to be based on the assumption that everyone can and should need/enjoy/ be good at everything that somebody else deemed important, is untenable. It does not suit everybody. Ideally we would have a state education system that delivers exactly what each and every individual student needs, to derive the most from the natural talents and abilities they were born with and/or are able to learn/develop.

We should encourage a desire to learn, and teach our children to think, not to pass tests.

At present we have extra provisions, and do our best to help, those children with special needs, or who are gifted and talented. But the way the latter are identified appears to be inconsistent and often inappropriate. I suppose this is a start towards a curriculum tailored to the individual, but what about the rest?

A customized personal learning regime is something ICT could enable, if the will, the time and the money were there. If effectively planned and managed, given the available extra preparation time to create, research and decide how to use learning materials on them, information and computing technology (ICT) has a lot to offer education, but it cannot and should not take the place of a good teacher where some form of interaction e.g. discussions, or an inspirational lecture is required. ICT is best employed as a 1-to-1 teaching tool, because it allows students to work at their own speed and ability. In my opinion it should be deployed sparingly in a 1-to-many dissemination of knowledge situation.

2. School Funding

Funding comes from so many sources (LEA, LSE, direct from central government, EU, etc.), applying different rules and formulas (based on big and often invalid assumptions), that is difficult to track how much it is, where it has come from, why and where it has gone. This is true at all levels, individual schools to nationwide. Probably too much has gone to some problem areas (inner city schools) and not enough to those in rural towns, and 'good' schools get more funding than 'bad' ones. Funding is unfair and is not based adequately on needs.

3. League Tables and 'value added'.

Every (open) system has to have a means of assessing its performance or else it will decline into entropy that much sooner. But the criteria and methods of measurement must be valid and reliable, and not open to misuse/abuse.

4. Exclusions

Let's give our head teachers the right (and the balls!) to exclude any child who persistently disrupts the education of his/her fellow classmates, without fear of 'retribution' from the DfES or the recalcitrant child's parents.

Some New(er) Ideas

1. Four Term Year

Why do we still have an unbalanced holiday system based on an agricultural economy? The four-term year is not new; N.E. Somerset tried to go that way. However they tried to do so unilaterally, which was a mistake because it did not fit with the practices of other authorities on teacher contracts. So, the scheme was abandoned.

Let us try again and have equal length terms as well! Pupils and teachers then might be better able to cope with term time. As with some other ideas presented here, many stakeholders need to be considered to achieve this, not the least of which are the examination boards and the universities. But it could be done.

2. Abolish Homework

Where does the belief that homework must be set, handed in and marked, come from? Most teachers do not want to do this, many pupils would be happy to miss out as well (this does not preclude the possibility of teachers suggesting further reading and research for those who want it). Who does want homework? Parents, maybe (something to keep the kids quiet in the evening/at weekends?), head teachers (not wishing to upset parents?). We should not need homework if education was effective during the daytime. Reliance on it to complete the learning disadvantages those children that do not come from a home background conducive to it.

Many teachers enjoy and do not begrudge the time they need to spend preparing their lessons and teaching materials, outside of normal teaching hours. It is the marking which is the 'killer'. We could get close to Estelle Morris' shorter working week for teachers if we abolished homework!

3. Languages

Instead of learning one foreign language (usually French) to a moderate standard, it might be better to teach just enough of many languages to get by as a visitor to the country. There might be scope for a comparative approach to language teaching – in the same way that religious instruction in Christianity only, has evolved into a comparative study of the major religions

We English are bad with languages; many of us do not bother to attempt to speak another language, because so many other nationalities can and do speak English. I would like to encourage an attitude that speaking a few words in the local language when abroad is simply a common courtesy.

Too much political intervention

Why must education be a political football? It is too important to be left to the whims of politicians seeking to get (re)elected. Education needs a longer strategic plan than the timing of the next General Election (or tomorrow's tabloids!). People are in the education system for at least 11 years, sometimes as many asto 18 years; they are entitled to a stable and consistent education policy over that period. Politicians' horizons are four to five years at the most.

Change should be gradual, and based on evidence-based testing, conservation of what is good in the old system, and thinking through the possible consequences, with input from those with relevant experience. The effectiveness of any change depends on the commitment of those who will have to implement it at the chalkface; it is essential to win their hearts and minds through genuine, respectful consultation and sharing of evidence. Governments (and their civil servants and political advisers) are sadly lacking in the expertise of successful change management

Monetary policy was judged to be too important to be left to politicians, so the Bank of England was asked to set up a Monetary Policy Committee of experts to operate the system, within broad policy parameters. It undertakes economic research as a basis for its decisions; it publishes the data and also the minutes of its meetings

Education policy is entitled to a similar insulation from day-to-day interference by government, following similar principles to the Monetary Policy Committee. The composition of the Education Policy Committee, its terms of reference and method of operation need careful thinking through and discussion with representatives of interested parties. Correctly implemented, the concept could bring musch needed stability and consistency into education policy.

Next time we have an educational problem, it would be good to get representatives of all affected parties (with the possible exception of politicians) to sit down together and do some creative problem solving. A mutually acceptable solution is possible if all parties want to achieve it and believe they can.

Many (possibly all) of the ideas presented here have flaws. I have not bothered to mention them, as I am sure you, the reader, have heard/identified most of them and are shouting them at me as you read this. Let's do some creative problemsolving to see if we can minimize/remove these flaws.

Michael J. Hicks has spent three years in secondary schools (teaching mathematics), four in further education (teaching maths., statistics, physics, computer science and electronic systems), and twenty three years in higher education at Slough College, which became a part of Thames Valley University (teaching mathematics, statistics/OR, strategic information systems and organizational behaviour). Having retired from full time university work, he is now a writer, trainer and consultant in creativity and innovation.

He is the author of Problem Solving and Decision Making: Hard, Soft and Creative Approaches, 2nd Edition, 2004, Thomson Learning, ISBN 1-86152-617-2

SYNECTICS EDUCATION INITIATIVE (SEI)

SEI is a Registered Charity dedicated to promoting the use of creativity and innovation techniques, particularly those developed in business, in the formal education system.

It was formed in 1990 as a result of positive results obtained from experiencing the Synectics techniques by educational psychologists and teachers working in schools and universities

Since its formation, SEI has
- Run a number of conferences, most recently the EXCITE! Project Conference in May 2004
- Delivered training courses for educational psychologists, teachers and universities, including an undergraduate course for Surrey University Chemical Engineering Department
- Managed the EXCITE! (Excellence, Creativity and Innovation in Teaching and Education) Project involving the training of groups of teachers in Norfolk, Bracknell Forest, Merseyside and Staffordshire. The programme was evaluated by a research team from the Open University
- Developed and run a pilot EXCITE! Train the Trainer programme to enable advisors and others to train teachers in their areas
- Developed and run a pilot Creative Science course for science teachers, on behalf of DfES and the Wellcome Trust
- Published Creative Education: Developing a Nation of Innovators, 2000
- Undertaken consultancy work for BT Education
- Led a bid to run an Education Action Zone in Aylesbury, Bucks

The current intention is to provide a support network and discussion forum for accredited EXCITE! Trainers via the SEI website, www.excite-education.org   SEI invites anyone who shares its objectives to become a member. Contact the Hon.Sec/Treasurer, Vincent Nolan, via the website or by email at vincentnolan@online.rednet.co.uk

OTHER PUBLICATIONS BY SEI

Creative Education: *Educating a Nation of Innovators*

Papers by Members of Synectics Education Initiative;
edited by Vincent Nolan
Synectics Education Initiative, 2000 ISBN 0 9538534 0
A5/240pp/Price £10.00 plus £1.50 post and packing

The experience of business in unlocking the creative and
innovative potential of its employees over the last 40 years
provides a tried and tested body of knowledge which can be
applied successfully to formal education in schools, colleges
and universities, as pilot projects have demonstrated.
The authors write from their experiences in business and
education.

"As the Chairman of NACCCE (the National Advisory Committee
on Creative and Cultural Education) I particularly welcome
publication of this book, which brings together the experience
of those who have been pioneering the use of these techniques.
The authors....present a mass of experiential evidence and
theoretical argument about the value of training in creative
techniques in education."
Professor Ken Robinson

"This book....gives concrete, practical advice on how to do new
things and bring innovation and creativity alive in education.
Some – mostly business – perspectives chip in an interesting
and fresh look at the challenges facing the education system,
while others are firmly rooted in educational experience. ...It is
not only intended for those interested in formal education, but
also for parents, students, employers, employees or anyone
committed to creativity and lifelong learning in general. It
is stuffed with easily readable, practical, useful real-life
situations which will certainly make everyone think."
From a review of the book by Mathilda Joubert, educational
creativity consultant, in the RSA Journal, 4/4 2000

EXCITE! *Report of the EXCITE! (Excellence, Creativity and Innovation in Teaching and Education) Project, 2004*
A4 62 pages, available in pdf format on
www.excite-education.org

This pilot project assessed the effect of creativity training based on the Synectics model for four groups of teachers in Norfolk, Bracknell Forest, Merseyside and Staffordshire and included an evaluation by a team from the Open University. The project was funded by the Esmee Fairbairn Foundation and the Department for Education and Skills

"To achieve an education-wide focus on creative teaching and learning, the role of the teacher needs to shift from a transmitter of knowledge to a facilitator of learning, through fostering the development of creative potential in all pupils.....
I believe that EXCITE!'s approach to foster creative teaching and learning in a practical way, brings us a step closer to that basic entitlement for all children"
Hilary Hodgson, Programme Director: Education, Esmee Fairbairn Foundation